The Wild Side

Bizarre Endings

The Wild Side
Bizarre Endings

Henry Billings
Melissa Billings

JAMESTOWN  PUBLISHERS

a division of NTC/Contemporary Publishing Group
Lincolnwood, Illinois USA

ISBN 0–8092-9511-3

Published by Jamestown Publishers,
a division of NTC/Contemporary Publishing Group, Inc.
4255 West Touhy Avenue
Lincolnwood (Chicago), Illinois 60712-1975, U.S.A.

00 01 02 03 04 VL 10 9 8 7 6 5 4 3 2 1

CONTENTS

UNIT THREE

To the Student

An old cliché warns us that you never can tell how things will turn out. Some events prove the truth of that warning spectacularly. An individual who has lived in a vegetative state for several years suddenly wakes up. An entire group of people, left on their own for a short period, vanishes. One person who has everything is unable to enjoy anything, while another who is dying thinks himself into good health. A person with talent, wealth, and fame loses his life to injustice; "nobodies" win worldwide fame by pretending to be "somebodies." A series of unfortunate happenings clings mysteriously to an object and to a place. And people become obsessed by tales of mysterious doings . . . where nothing at all is out of the ordinary.

As you read and enjoy the 15 articles in this book, you will be developing your reading skills. If you complete all the lessons in this book, you will surely increase your reading speed and improve your reading comprehension and critical thinking skills. Also, because these exercises include items of the types often found on state and national tests, learning how to complete them will prepare you for tests you may have to take in the future.

How to Use This Book

About the Book.   *Bizarre Endings* contains three units, each of which includes five lessons. Each lesson begins with an article about an unusual subject or event. The article is followed by a group of four reading comprehension exercises and three critical thinking exercises. The reading comprehension exercises will help you understand the article. The critical thinking exercises will help you think about what you have read and how it relates to your own experience.

At the end of each lesson, you will also have the opportunity to give your personal response to some aspect of the article and then to assess how well you understood what you read.

The Sample Lesson.   Working through the sample lesson, the first lesson in the book, with your class or group will demonstrate how a lesson is organized. The sample lesson explains how to complete the exercises and score your answers. The correct answers for the sample exercises and sample scores are printed in lighter type. In some cases, explanations of the correct answers are given. The explanations will help you understand how to think through these question types.

If you have any questions about how to complete the exercises or score them, this is the time to get the answers.

Working Through Each Lesson.   Begin each lesson by looking at the photograph and reading the caption. Before you read, predict what you think the article will be about. Then read the article.

Sometimes your teacher may decide to time your reading. Timing helps you keep track of and increase your reading speed. If you have been timed, enter your reading time in the box at the end of the lesson. Then use the Words-per-Minute Table to find your reading speed, and record your speed on the Reading Speed graph at the end of the unit.

Next complete the Reading Comprehension and Critical Thinking exercises. The directions for each exercise will tell you how to mark your answers. When you have finished all four Reading Comprehension exercises, use the answer key provided by your teacher to check your work. Follow the directions after each exercise to find your score. Record your Reading Comprehension scores on the graph at the end of each unit. Then check your answers to the Author's Approach, Summarizing and Paraphrasing, and Critical Thinking exercises. Fill in the Critical Thinking Chart at the end of each unit with your evaluation of your work and comments about your progress.

At the end of each unit you will also complete a Compare and Contrast Chart. The completed chart will help you see what the articles have in common, and it will give you an opportunity to explore your own ideas about the events in the articles.

SAMPLE LESSON

What Happened to Jimmy Hoffa?

Some people adored him. Other people despised him. With Jimmy Hoffa, there seemed to be no middle ground. In 1957 Hoffa became president of the Teamsters, a union of truckers. He ruled the union with an iron fist.

Hoffa demanded high wages for his people. That made many members love him. But his enemies claimed he was ruthless. Anyone who crossed him had to watch out. They might be beaten up or harassed in other ways.

2   Hoffa's enemies were right. Hoffa was more than a union leader. He was

A happy Jimmy Hoffa smiles at reporters as he leaves a federal prison after serving part of his sentence. Four years later, he disappeared without a trace. Was Hoffa murdered? If so, why was his body never found?

also a crook. He had close ties to "the mob," or organized crime. More than once, the federal government tried to prove that Hoffa was corrupt and was taking advantage of his union. At last, in 1964, Hoffa lost two trials. He was found guilty of tampering with a jury. He was also found guilty of taking union money for his own use. Hoffa made several appeals. But he lost them all. In 1967 he began to serve a 13-year sentence in prison.

3   Hoffa did not just roll over and play dead, though. He found a way to run the Teamsters from behind bars. He used his son, James, as a go-between. "He was like a caged lion in prison," said James later. "All he talked about was his union."

4   In 1971 Hoffa was paroled. After serving just four years of his sentence, he was freed. But there was a string attached to his freedom. He could not hold any union office for nine years. (That was the time left on his sentence.) This deal had been set up by Frank Fitzsimmons, the union's vice president.

5   It is not clear why Fitzsimmons acted as he did. Maybe he was just

trying to help Hoffa. Or maybe he was trying to limit Hoffa's power. In any case, Hoffa did not know about the deal until after he was free. He hated it. He felt Fitzsimmons had double-crossed him.

6   Hoffa spent the next four years trying to get the ban lifted. He fought Fitzsimmons for control of the Teamsters. Some members of the mob supported Hoffa. Others threw their support to Fitzsimmons.

7   On July 30, 1975, Hoffa planned to meet some gangsters for lunch. He hoped to win their support in his fight with Fitzsimmons. The men were supposed to meet at a restaurant near Detroit. Hoffa got there first. He waited patiently, but the gangsters never showed up. After a few hours, Hoffa called home. Had they left a message for him? They had not. One witness saw Hoffa leave the restaurant. He was in the back seat of a car with some other men. It was the last time anyone ever saw the 62-year-old union leader.

8   Hoffa's son, James, remembered what happened the next morning. "My mother called about 6:30 A.M. She

told me that [my father] hadn't come home. Right away I expected the worst." In other words, James believed his father had been killed.

9   The police agreed. But they had no proof. Hoffa's body was never found. At first, the police got lots of tips. They looked for his body everywhere. They dug up cornfields. They drilled through concrete floors. They checked rivers and lakes. But their searches always came up empty.

10   Meanwhile, weird rumors about Hoffa kept floating about. Some people believed that the mob had cut up his body and dropped the pieces in a swamp. Others claimed he was buried under the goalposts at Giants Stadium in New Jersey. Still others said his body was put in a car crusher. The best bet might be that his killers dropped him into a vat of boiling zinc. That was how the Detroit mob often got rid of a murder victim.

11   Only the killers know the true story. But none of them are talking. And unless one of them does talk, the rest of us will never know what really happened to Jimmy Hoffa.

If you have been timed while reading this article, enter your reading time below. Then turn to the Words-per-Minute Table on page 55 and look up your reading speed (words per minute). Enter your reading speed on the graph on page 56.

Reading Time: Sample Lesson

———— : ————
Minutes   Seconds

A Finding the Main Idea

One statement below expresses the main idea of the article. One statement is too general, or too broad. The other statement explains only part of the article; it is too narrow. Label the statements using the following key:

M—Main Idea   **B—Too Broad**   **N—Too Narrow**

_B_ 1. None of Jimmy Hoffa's thousands of followers could have predicted what would happen to Hoffa. [This statement is true, but too broad. It doesn't make clear who Hoffa was or what happened to him.]

_N_ 2. After losing two trials and many appeals, Jimmy Hoffa began serving a 13-year prison sentence. [This statement is too narrow. It presents only details.]

_M_ 3. After being jailed for crimes against his labor union, Jimmy Hoffa disappeared while seeking gangster help to regain control of the union. [This is the main idea. It tells whom the story is about and what part of his life is discussed.]

_____ Score 15 points for a correct M answer.

_____ Score 5 points for each correct B or N answer.

_____ **Total Score:** Finding the Main Idea

B Recalling Facts

How well do you remember the facts in the article? Put an X in the box next to the answer that correctly completes each statement about the article.

1. Jimmy Hoffa was the president of
☐ a. organized crime in Detroit.
☒ b. the Teamsters, a union of truckers.
☐ c. an automobile company.

2. Hoffa was sent to prison for
☒ a. taking union money for his own use.
☐ b. using his son as a go-between.
☐ c. having his enemies beaten up.

3. While in prison, Hoffa
☐ a. made new deals with gangsters there.
☒ b. still ran the Teamsters.
☐ c. worked out a deal for his own parole.

4. In 1971 Hoffa was paroled on one condition: that he could not hold any union office
☐ a. higher than local representative.
☐ b. for the rest of his life.
☒ c. for nine more years.

5. Hoffa was last seen alive
☐ a. in a Detroit restaurant.
☐ b. at Giants Stadium in New Jersey.
☒ c. in the back seat of a car near Detroit.

Score 5 points for each correct answer.

_25_ **Total Score:** Recalling Facts

C Making Inferences

When you combine your own experience and information from a text to draw a conclusion that is not directly stated in that text, you are making an inference. Below are five statements that may or may not be inferences based on information in the article. Label the statements using the following key:

C—Correct Inference   F—Faulty Inference

__C__ 1. Some Teamsters didn't mind Hoffa's illegal acts as long as he could get good wages for the workers. [This is a *correct* inference. It was known that he had enemies beaten, yet many union members loved him.]

__F__ 2. The only reason Hoffa wanted control of the union was so that he could steal from it. [This is a *faulty* inference. There is no proof against other reasons, such as love of power or even interest in workers. Also, he could steal without having control.]

__C__ 3. Hoffa did not realize his life was in danger. [This is a *correct* inference. He went to the restaurant alone.]

__F__ 4. With Hoffa out of the picture, the Teamsters had no more connections to organized crime. [This is a *faulty* inference. Some mob members had thrown their support to the union's vice president.]

__F__ 5. No other unions have mob connections. [This is a *faulty* inference. Nothing in the story supports it.]

Score 5 points for each correct answer.

__25__ **Total Score:** Making Inferences

D Using Words Precisely

Each numbered sentence below contains an underlined word or phrase from the article. Following the sentence are three definitions. One definition is closest to the meaning of the underlined word. One definition is opposite or nearly opposite. Label those two definitions using the following key; do not label the remaining definition.

C—Closest   O—Opposite or Nearly Opposite

1. Some people <u>adored</u> him. Other people despised him.

_____ a. avoided

__C__ b. hated

__O__ c. loved

2. They might be beaten up or <u>harassed</u> in other ways.

__O__ a. comforted

__C__ b. annoyed repeatedly

_____ c. struck

3. He was found guilty of <u>tampering</u> with a jury.

_____ a. lying to

__O__ b. upholding; supporting

__C__ c. interfering with; bothering

4. He was also found <u>guilty</u> of taking union money for his own use.

__C__ a. to blame for

__O__ b. innocent of

_____ c. enthusiastic about

5. He felt Fitzsimmons had <u>double-crossed</u> him.

_____0_____ a. protected

_____ b. disgraced

_____C_____ c. betrayed

_____15_____ Score 3 points for each correct C answer.

_____10_____ Score 2 points for each correct O answer.

_____25_____ **Total Score:** Using Words Precisely

Enter the four total scores in the spaces below, and add them together to find your Reading Comprehension Score. Then record your score on the graph on page 57.

Score	Question Type	Sample Lesson
25	Finding the Main Idea	
25	Recalling Facts	
25	Making Inferences	
25	Using Words Precisely	
100	**Reading Comprehension Score**	

Author's Approach

Put an X in the box next to the correct answer.

1. What do the authors mean by the statement, "He ruled the union with an iron fist"?

☐ a. He had only one hand; he lost the other hand in an accident.

☒ b. He was a tough leader.

☐ c. He had been a champion boxer before he took over the union.

2. Judging by statements from the article "What Happened to Jimmy Hoffa?" you can conclude that the authors want the reader to think that

☐ a. Jimmy Hoffa probably escaped from gangsters and is now in hiding.

☒ b. Jimmy Hoffa was probably murdered by gangsters.

☐ c. Jimmy Hoffa probably faked his own death and is living in another country.

3. From the statements below, choose those that you believe the authors would agree with.

☒ a. Jimmy Hoffa was sometimes willing to break the law when it would help him and his union.

☐ b. Jimmy Hoffa was an innocent victim of evil people.

☒ c. It wouldn't be surprising if Hoffa was murdered by gangsters, since he had made many enemies.

_____3_____ Number of correct answers

Record your personal assessment of your work on the Critical Thinking Chart on page 58.

Summarizing and Paraphrasing

Put an X in the box next to the correct answer.

1. Below are summaries of the article. Choose the summary that says all the most important things about the article, but in the fewest words.

   ☐ a. Jimmy Hoffa was a powerful leader in the United States. [This summary leaves out almost all of the important details, such as what organization Jimmy Hoffa led and what happened to him.]

   ☐ b. In 1957 Jimmy Hoffa became leader of the Teamsters union and made many enemies. Hoffa disappeared after waiting for gangsters at a restaurant. Police looked for his body everywhere, including in cornfields and under concrete floors. [This summary presents important ideas from the article but includes too many unnecessary details.]

   ☒ c. Jimmy Hoffa, a tough and sometimes ruthless union leader, disappeared in 1975. It could be that he was the victim of gangsters, although no one knows for sure, since his body has never been found. [This summary says all the most important things about the article in the fewest words.]

2. Read the statement from the article below. Then read the paraphrase of that statement. Choose the reason that best tells why the paraphrase does not say the same thing as the statement.

   Statement: Fitzsimmons might have been trying to help Hoffa, or he might have been trying to make him less powerful.

   Paraphrase: As Hoffa's friend, Fitzsimmons may have been trying to help the union leader.

   ☐ a. Paraphrase says too much.

   ☒ b. Paraphrase doesn't say enough. [This statement leaves out the possibility that Fitzsimmons was trying to limit Hoffa's power.]

   ☐ c. Paraphrase doesn't agree with the statement.

__2__ Number of correct answers

Record your personal assessment of your work on the Critical Thinking Chart on page 58.

Critical Thinking

Follow the directions provided for questions 1, 2, and 3. Put an X in the box next to the correct answer for the other questions.

1. For each statement below, write O if it expresses an opinion or write F if it expresses a fact.

   __F__ a. Jimmy Hoffa served four years of his prison sentence.

   __O__ b. People who do business with gangsters should expect to be double-crossed.

   __F__ c. In 1964 Jimmy Hoffa was found guilty of tampering with a jury and stealing union money.

2. Choose from the letters below to correctly complete the following statement. Write the letters on the lines.

On the positive side, ___*c*___, but on the negative side, ___*b*___.

a. Jimmy Hoffa was looking for support when he went to the restaurant on July 30, 1975

b. Jimmy Hoffa was probably murdered

c. Jimmy Hoffa, a convicted crook, is no longer running the Teamsters

3. Reread paragraph 8. Then choose from the letters below to correctly complete the following statement. Write the letters on the lines.

According to paragraph 8, ___*c*___ because ___*b*___.

a. James Hoffa remembered what happened on July 31, 1975

b. Jimmy Hoffa didn't come home the night before

c. James Hoffa concluded that his father had been killed

4. Of the following theme categories, which would this story fit into?

☐ a. If you play with fire, you might get burned.

☐ b. A friend in need is a friend indeed.

☒ c. Crime doesn't pay.

5. What did you have to do to answer question 3?

☒ a. find a cause (why something happened)

☐ b. find an opinion (what someone thinks about something)

☐ c. make a prediction (what might happen next)

___5___ Number of correct answers

Record your personal assessment of your work on the Critical Thinking Chart on page 58.

Personal Response

Would you recommend this article to other students? Explain.

___[Decide whether or not you would recommend this article to your friends.___

___On the lines, write reasons why you liked or disliked it.]___

_____

_____

Self-Assessment

I'm proud of the way I answered question _____ in the_____

section because _____

___[Choose one answer from the exercises that you think you answered___

___particularly well. Tell why you are proud of either your answer or the___

___process by which you reached it.]___

Self-Assessment

To get the most out of the *Wild Side* series, you need to take charge of your own progress in improving your reading comprehension and critical thinking skills. Here are some of the features that help you work on those essential skills.

Reading Comprehension Exercises. Complete these exercises immediately after reading the article. They help you recall what you have read, understand the stated and implied main ideas, and add words to your working vocabulary.

Critical Thinking Skills Exercises. These exercises help you focus on the authors' approach and purpose, recognize and generate summaries and paraphrases, and identify relationships between ideas.

Personal Response and Self-assessment. Questions in this category help you relate the articles to your personal experience and give you the opportunity to evaluate your understanding of the information in that lesson.

Compare and Contrast Charts. At the end of each unit you will complete a Compare and Contrast Chart. The completed chart helps you see what the articles have in common and gives you an opportunity to explore your own ideas about the topics discussed in the articles.

The Graphs. The graphs and charts at the end of each unit enable you to keep track of your progress. Check your graphs regularly with your teacher. Decide whether your progress is satisfactory or whether you need additional work on some skills. What types of exercises are you having difficulty with? Talk with your teacher about ways to work on the skills in which you need the most practice.

UNIT ONE

The Truth About the Tasaday

Could a Stone Age tribe survive into the 20th century? It didn't seem possible. By 1970 almost every place on Earth had been fully explored. How could any group be living unnoticed by the rest of the world? But in 1971 an amazing thing happened. A Stone Age tribe was found. The name of the tribe was the Tasaday. Experts everywhere were thrilled by this discovery.

2   How did the Tasaday stay unknown for so long? First, the tribe was tiny. It contained just 26 people.

In this picture Philippine official Manuel Elizalde (in white shirt) learns about the peaceful ways of a primitive tribe of people called the Tasaday, with the help of a local interpreter. These happy people seemed too good to be true—for a very good reason.

Second, they lived in deep caves. Third, their home was in a rain forest deep in the Philippines. And fourth, they made all the things they needed, so they had no reason to seek outside trading partners.

3   The Tasaday were discovered by a local trapper. He said he came upon them one day while hunting. The trapper told Manuel Elizalde, a Philippine official. Soon the word got out. Several experts came to see the tribe. They were eager to study the Tasaday. After all, these people knew nothing about the modern world. Visiting them was like traveling back in time. It allowed researchers to see how humans had lived long, long ago.

4   *National Geographic* fell in love with the Tasaday. The magazine did several stories on the tribe as it "stepped out of the Stone Age." Then came books, movies, and TV specials. Everyone, it seemed, adored these innocent people.

5   What were the Tasaday like? They wore very little clothing. What they did wear they wove from tree leaves. They did not know how to grow their own food. They had never seen rice, corn, or sugar. One expert said they could be "the only people in the world today who do not know or use tobacco." The Tasaday kept no domestic animals, either. They survived by eating wild palms, yams, crabs, and tadpoles. And, of course, the Tasaday had no metal. That is why they were called "Stone Age" people. Their only tools came from stone.

6   The Tasaday were very peaceful. Their sweet nature won the hearts of all those who saw them. The tribe had no words for "weapon" or "war" or "enemy." As one writer put it, "If our ancestors were like the Tasaday, we came from far better stock than I believed." It seemed that these Stone Age people might have a lot to teach the rest of us.

7   The goal, then, was to protect the Tasaday. That was Elizalde's job. He was in charge of protecting all the tribes in the Philippines. He did not want the Tasaday's way of life ruined. He feared that would happen if too many people came to visit. So he sent soldiers to guard the caves. Just a few people were allowed in. And first they had to be approved by Elizalde. Because of this rule, few scientists got to see the tribe.

And that's the way things stayed until 1986.

8   Meanwhile, the Tasaday seemed to look on Elizalde as a god. "Our ancestors told us never to leave this place of ours," said one. "They told us the god of our people would come. Their words have been proven true by the coming of [Elizalde]." The Tasaday even gave him a new name. It was Mono Dakel de Weta Tasaday. That meant "Great Man, God of the Tasaday."

9   But as time passed, rumors began to spread. Some people started to have doubts about the tribe. One person claimed he saw cooked rice being sneaked into the caves. Others said they saw the Tasaday wearing clothes. Still others maintained they had seen tribe members smoking cigarettes. Few people listened to these reports, however. Belief in the "Stone Age" tribe ran too deep.

10   Then, in 1986, a huge change took place in the Philippines. The old government was swept away. A new, freer one was set up. Even before the old regime ended, Elizalde slipped out of sight. He simply vanished. It was

said that he fled the country. He took $35 million with him. It was money that he was supposed to have used to aid tribes like the Tasaday.

11   When the old government crumbled, so did the shield around the Tasaday. Now outsiders could see for themselves who these people really were. A Swiss writer named Oswald Iten went looking for the Tasaday. He found their caves empty. He did, however, find the very same "Stone Age" people a short distance away. They were living in comfortable huts. They were wearing T-shirts and jeans. And they were using metal knives.

12   Iten realized that the whole tribe was nothing but a hoax. The people claiming to be Tasaday really came from two other tribes. These tribes had been part of the modern world for many, many years.

13   Soon others picked up the story. ABC did a TV special. It was called "The Tribe That Never Was." It showed the Tasaday laughing as they looked at photos of themselves from *National Geographic*. Tasaday supporters now

faced tough questions. Why were the caves so clean? Where were the crab shells and scraps of food? Even Stone Age tribes had garbage, didn't they?

14   Besides, how could such a small tribe sustain itself? Wouldn't the Tasaday have needed spouses from the outside? Scientists said a tribe living on its own would need at least 400 members, not 26. The Tasaday said they sometimes married people from two other Stone Age tribes. But these other tribes were never found.

15   Finally, the Tasaday caves were just a three-hour walk from an established village. How come no one from the tribe ever walked there? Had their search for food never brought them near the village? It made no sense—unless the tribe was a fake. One expert called the Tasaday "rain forest clock punchers." They went to work as "cave people" in the morning. At night, after the visitors left, they went back to their village homes.

16   Who was behind this fraud? The finger points to Elizalde. He made lots of money from his scheme to

"protect" the Tasaday. The "Tasaday" agreed to go along with him because they were poor. They were told they could make some money by putting on a show. "Elizalde said if we went naked we'd get [money] because we'd look poor," one man explained.

17   The Tasaday put on a great act. They fooled everyone for a while. Even the so-called experts fell for the scam. But we now know that the Tasaday are not a real Stone Age tribe. If such a tribe does still exist, no one has found it yet.

If you have been timed while reading this article, enter your reading time below. Then turn to the Words-per-Minute Table on page 55 and look up your reading speed (words per minute). Enter your reading speed on the graph on page 56.

Reading Time: Lesson 1

——— : ———
Minutes   Seconds

A Finding the Main Idea

One statement below expresses the main idea of the article. One statement is too general, or too broad. The other statement explains only part of the article; it is too narrow. Label the statements using the following key:

M—Main Idea   **B—Too Broad**   **N—Too Narrow**

_____ 1. Even researchers and scientists can be misled when they allow their desire to make remarkable discoveries overcome common sense.

_____ 2. The apparent discovery of a Stone Age tribe in the Philippines in 1971 was revealed to be a hoax just 15 years later.

_____ 3. Manuel Elizalde, a Philippine official, said that he was protecting a small, primitive tribe from being confused by the modern world.

_____ Score 15 points for a correct M answer.

_____ Score 5 points for each correct B or N answer.

_____ **Total Score:** Finding the Main Idea

B Recalling Facts

How well do you remember the facts in the article? Put an X in the box next to the answer that correctly completes each statement about the article.

1. The Tasaday tribe was reported to be discovered by a
   □ a. visiting scientist.
   □ b. government official.
   □ c. local trapper.

2. Observers said the Tasaday ate such things as
   □ a. wild palms, yams, crabs, and tadpoles.
   □ b. rice, corn, and sugar.
   □ c. cheese, eggs, and bacon.

3. Manuel Elizalde was given the job of protecting
   □ a. the Tasaday from land grabbers.
   □ b. all Philippine tribes from researchers and too rapid change.
   □ c. researchers from the Tasaday.

4. After the old government crumbled,
   □ a. a Swiss writer discovered the Tasaday hoax.
   □ b. Manuel Elizalde was arrested.
   □ c. the Tasaday had to pay back the money the government had given them.

5. A clue to the hoax that had been ignored was that
   □ a. the Tasaday cooked rice in their caves.
   □ b. Tasaday caves had no garbage in them.
   □ c. the tribe was too large to be unseen for so long.

Score 5 points for each correct answer.

_____ **Total Score:** Recalling Facts

C Making Inferences

When you combine your own experience and information from a text to draw a conclusion that is not directly stated in that text, you are making an inference. Below are five statements that may or may not be inferences based on information in the article. Label the statements using the following key:

C—Correct Inference   **F—Faulty Inference**

_____ 1. A fairly large amount of land in the Philippines is covered with rain forest.

_____ 2. Scientists of today know rather little about the daily life of people in the Stone Age.

_____ 3. All officials in the old Philippine government were dishonest.

_____ 4. Swiss writers are more careful in their research than other writers.

_____ 5. If researchers had not been carried away by the idea of making a great discovery, they could have seen from the start that the Tasaday tribe was a fake.

Score 5 points for each correct answer.

_____ **Total Score:** Making Inferences

D Using Words Precisely

Each numbered sentence below contains an underlined word or phrase from the article. Following the sentence are three definitions. One definition is closest to the meaning of the underlined word. One definition is opposite or nearly opposite. Label those two definitions using the following key; do not label the remaining definition.

C—Closest   **O—Opposite or Nearly Opposite**

1. Everyone, it seemed, adored these <u>innocent</u> people.

_____ a. dishonest; not sincere

_____ b. natural; simple

_____ c. intelligent; smart

2. The Tasaday kept no <u>domestic</u> animals, either.

_____ a. large

_____ b. wild

_____ c. tame

3. As one writer put it, "If our <u>ancestors</u> were like the Tasaday, we came from far better stock than I believed."

_____ a. those from whom one is descended

_____ b. neighbors

_____ c. descendants

4. Besides, how could such a small tribe <u>sustain</u> itself? Wouldn't the Tasaday have needed spouses from the outside?

_____ a. end; put a stop to

_____ b. amuse; entertain

_____ c. maintain; keep going

5. Finally, the Tasaday caves were just a three-hour walk from an <u>established</u> village.

_____ a. modern; up-to-date

_____ b. permanent

_____ c. undependable; changing

_____ Score 3 points for each correct C answer.

_____ Score 2 points for each correct O answer.

_____ **Total Score:** Using Words Precisely

Enter the four total scores in the spaces below, and add them together to find your Reading Comprehension Score. Then record your score on the graph on page 57.

Score	Question Type	Lesson 1
_____	Finding the Main Idea	
_____	Recalling Facts	
_____	Making Inferences	
_____	Using Words Precisely	
_____	**Reading Comprehension Score**	

Author's Approach

Put an X in the box next to the correct answer.

1. The main purpose of the first paragraph is to

☐ a. introduce readers to the topic of the article.

☐ b. describe the Tasaday tribe.

☐ c. point out how easily people can be fooled.

2. Which of the following statements from the article best describes conditions under which the Tasaday people seemed to live?

☐ a. The Tasaday were discovered by a local trapper.

☐ b. Their sweet nature won the hearts of all those who saw them.

☐ c. They survived by eating wild palms, yams, crabs, and tadpoles. And, of course, the Tasaday had no metal.

3. Judging by statements from the article "The Truth About the Tasaday," you can conclude that the authors want the reader to think that

☐ a. no one ever truly believed the Tasaday were Stone Age people.

☐ b. many people were fooled by the story of the Tasaday.

☐ c. only Manuel Elizalde knew that the Tasaday were fakes.

4. The authors tell this story mainly by

☐ a. comparing different topics.

☐ b. telling different stories about the same topic.

☐ c. telling about events in the order they happened.

_____ Number of correct answers

Record your personal assessment of your work on the Critical Thinking Chart on page 58.

Summarizing and Paraphrasing

Follow the directions provided for question 1. Put an X in the box next to the correct answer for the other questions.

1. Look for the important ideas and events in paragraphs 3 and 4. Summarize those paragraphs in one or two sentences.

_____

_____

_____

2. Read the statement from the article below. Then read the paraphrase of that statement. Choose the reason that best tells why the paraphrase does not say the same thing as the statement.

   Statement: In 1986 Elizalde vanished, taking $35 million meant for the Tasaday with him.

   Paraphrase: Elizalde disappeared in 1986.

   ☐ a. Paraphrase says too much.

   ☐ b. Paraphrase doesn't say enough.

   ☐ c. Paraphrase doesn't agree with the statement.

3. Choose the sentence that correctly restates the following sentence from the article: "When the old government crumbled, so did the shield around the Tasaday."

   ☐ a. The Tasaday were no longer protected from curious people after the government fell.

   ☐ b. The Tasaday erected a shield to protect themselves after the government crumbled.

   ☐ c. The Tasaday and the government were both protected by the same shield, so when it crumbled, they both suffered.

_____ Number of correct answers

Record your personal assessment of your work on the Critical Thinking Chart on page 58.

Critical Thinking

Follow the directions provided for question 1. Put an X in the box next to the correct answer for the other questions.

1. For each statement below, write *O* if it expresses an opinion or write *F* if it expresses a fact.

   _____ a. The people involved in the Tasaday hoax should be ashamed of themselves.

   _____ b. Everyone would have known that the Tasaday were a fraud if more reporters had been allowed to interview them.

   _____ c. In 1986 there was a change in the government of the Philippines.

2. From what happened in the article, you can predict that if anyone else ever reports having found a Stone Age tribe,

☐ a. all scientists will ignore the news because they don't want to be fooled again.

☐ b. no one will believe the story.

☐ c. scientists and reporters will check the facts more carefully.

3. What was the effect of the crumbling of the Philippine government?

☐ a. Elizalde began to persuade the Tasaday to talk to reporters.

☐ b. The Tasaday started wearing T-shirts and blue jeans.

☐ c. The Tasaday could no longer be hidden from the public.

4. Of the following theme categories, which would this story fit into?

☐ a. It is difficult to keep up a lie for very long.

☐ b. No one profits by a lie.

☐ c. It is wise to demand concrete proof before you believe an outlandish story.

5. What did you have to do to answer question 2?

☐ a. find an opinion (what someone thinks about something)

☐ b. make a prediction (what might happen next)

☐ c. draw a conclusion (a sensible statement based on the text and your experience)

_____ Number of correct answers

Record your personal assessment of your work on the Critical Thinking Chart on page 58.

Personal Response

A question I would like answered by Manuel Elizalde is _____

_____

_____

_____

Self-Assessment

One of the things I did best when reading this article was _____

_____

_____

I believe I did this well because _____

_____

_____

Lost for 16 Years

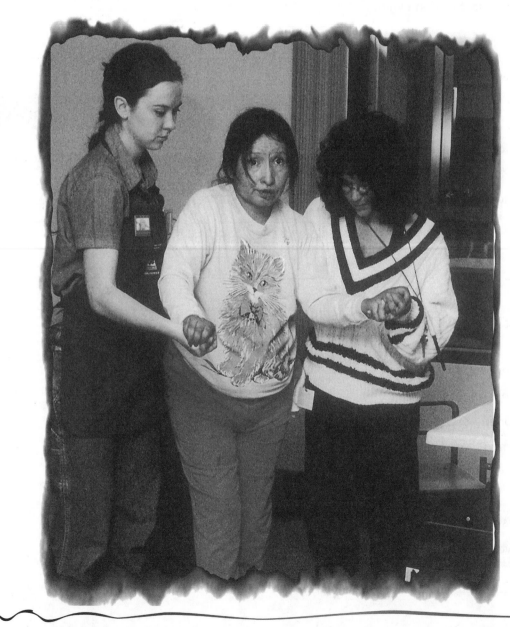

Patti White Bull checked into the hospital on June 12, 1983. "I'll see you tomorrow," she told her nine-year-old daughter, Cindy. By then, Patti thought, she would have given birth to her fourth child. She would be able to show Cindy a brand new brother or sister.

2   Patti and her husband, Mark, already had three children. Besides Cindy, there were three-year-old Jesse and one-year-old Floris. So while Patti went to the hospital in Albuquerque, New Mexico, Mark cared for the three children. That night he took them to work with him.

How would it feel to wake up after 16 years in a coma? Less than two months after her recovery, Patti White Bull tests her ability to walk with the help of a volunteer and a physical therapist.

3   By the next morning, Mark was eager to join Patti. But first he had to make a quick stop at their house in Edgewood. There, Mark found a note pinned to the door. That was when he learned something had gone wrong.

4   Patti had given birth to a healthy baby boy. But a blood clot had formed. It lodged in her lung. That caused her to stop breathing. Her heart stopped pumping oxygen to her brain. Doctors scrambled to save her. But it took six minutes to get her breathing again. By then she was in a coma. She could not respond to the people around her. She was unconscious.

5   Mark hoped Patti would come out of the coma quickly. But after a few days, her condition had not changed. Sadly, Mark brought Cindy to the hospital to see Patti. Cindy was shocked. She thought of her 27-year-old mother as a beautiful and active woman. Patti White Bull had worked as a model. She had made jewelry and taught yoga. A member of the Pueblo tribe, she had also worked to help other Native Americans. In fact, she had been so upbeat that her nickname was Happi.

6   But now tubes were sticking out of Patti's body. Her eyes were open, but vacant. She did not appear to see anything. She didn't even blink. She could not swallow, so she was being fed through a tube. Her hands were tightly clenched. No part of her body moved.

7   Cindy White Bull was crushed. So was Mark. He asked his mother to care for the new baby, named Mark, Jr. Mark and the other children spent many nights sleeping in the bathroom of Patti's hospital room. They all wanted to be there if she woke up.

8   But the days passed and Patti did not stir. She was moved to the Las Palomas Nursing Home. There she remained locked in what doctors called a semi-vegetative state. For two years Mark visited her almost every day. "Sometimes I would try to talk her into waking up," he said. "I'd say, 'You're by a stream now. We're sitting together. You're really tired, but you need to wake up now. The kids need you. I need you. . . .' "

9   It didn't work. By 1985 Patti still showed no sign of improvement. Finally, Mark decided he had to move on with his life. He asked the courts to grant him a divorce. Then he moved to South Dakota. There his mother could help him raise his children.

10   It was hard for everyone to leave Patti behind. But the doctors said that she wouldn't know the difference. She could not hear them. She could not see them. Doctors expected her to spend the rest of her life in a catatonic state.

11   As the years passed, Mark White Bull struggled to forget Patti. He married and divorced two more times. Meanwhile Cindy and her siblings grew up. In 1989 Cindy joined the Marines. By 1999 she was married and had children of her own. Jesse was in college. Floris and Mark, Jr., were teenagers. None of them thought they would ever see their mother awake again.

12   But four days before Christmas, an amazing thing happened. A nurse's aide was fixing the sheets on Patti's bed when all at once Patti spoke. "Don't do that!" she exclaimed.

13   No one at the nursing home could believe it. After 16 years Patti White Bull had woken up.

14 Within hours Patti was on the phone to her mother. Her voice was shaky but clear. "Merry Christmas, Mom," she said.

15 It took a while to reach the rest of the family. When Mark White Bull heard the news, he quickly made plans to drive to New Mexico. Jesse, Floris, and Mark, Jr., went with him. Cindy was away on vacation. But when she heard what had happened, she, too, left for New Mexico.

16 By Christmas morning Patti was able to dress herself. With a little help she could take a few steps. Later that week, when Cindy arrived, Patti held out her arms for a hug.

17 "Her face was lit up," said Cindy.

18 When Mark, Jr., arrived Patti murmured, "Junior?" It was the first time he had ever heard her voice.

19 Patti's muscles and vocal chords were very weak. In addition, she showed some signs of brain damage. She needed to learn many things all over again. She couldn't brush her hair or wash her hands by herself. Still, it was astounding to see what she could do. Within a couple of weeks, she took her first bite of pizza. She tried on some lipstick. Best of all, she gave all her children big hugs.

20 Dr. Eliot Marcus was in charge of Patti's case. "I cannot come up with a medical explanation," he said. "I have never seen anything like this." Other doctors said the same thing. "It really is quite amazing," said one. Another simply called it "absolutely extraordinary."

21 To this day no one knows what caused Patti White Bull to wake up. But some doctors have a theory. In December 1999 the flu was going around Patti's nursing home. To protect the patients, doctors gave out a flu medicine. It was called amantadine. Patti White Bull was given some of it. Perhaps this medicine somehow triggered her recovery.

22 Once Patti woke up, doctors kept giving her amantadine. They feared that without it, she would go downhill. Even with it, they were not sure what her future held. They warned the family that she could slip back into a coma at any time. But the family was happy just to take one day at a time. As Patti's son Jesse said, "Every moment with her is a special moment for me and my brother and sisters. It's something we never had. When you find it, you want to hold it as long as you can."

If you have been timed while reading this article, enter your reading time below. Then turn to the Words-per-Minute Table on page 55 and look up your reading speed (words per minute). Enter your reading speed on the graph on page 56.

Reading Time: Lesson 2

———— : ————
Minutes   Seconds

A Finding the Main Idea

One statement below expresses the main idea of the article. One statement is too general, or too broad. The other statement explains only part of the article; it is too narrow. Label the statements using the following key:

M—Main Idea   **B—Too Broad**   **N—Too Narrow**

_____ 1. In 1983 a woman suddenly went into a coma during childbirth. Sixteen years later, she unexpectedly awoke from her coma to greet her family.

_____ 2. For 16 years Mark White Bull and his four children hoped that Patti White Bull would wake from the coma she slipped into after a blood clot lodged in her lung.

_____ 3. Giving birth to a child can be more dangerous than most people realize.

_____ Score 15 points for a correct M answer.

_____ Score 5 points for each correct B or N answer.

_____ **Total Score:** Finding the Main Idea

B Recalling Facts

How well do you remember the facts in the article? Put an X in the box next to the answer that correctly completes each statement about the article.

1. Patti White Bull went into a coma after
☐ a. a terrible auto accident.
☐ b. the birth of her fourth child.
☐ c. a bad fall.

2. One job that Patti had not done before falling into a coma was
☐ a. driving a truck.
☐ b. teaching yoga.
☐ c. working as a model.

3. In 1985 Mark White Bull, Patti's husband,
☐ a. fell into a coma too.
☐ b. divorced Patti and moved.
☐ c. died.

4. Patti finally woke up
☐ a. when her daughter Cindy had her first child.
☐ b. just before Christmas in 1985.
☐ c. four days before Christmas in 1999.

5. Patti may have regained consciousness because
☐ a. her body was reacting to a flu shot.
☐ b. she heard a loud noise in the nursing home.
☐ c. a nurse moved her roughly.

Score 5 points for each correct answer.

_____ **Total Score:** Recalling Facts

C | Making Inferences

When you combine your own experience with information from a text to draw a conclusion that is not directly stated in that text, you are making an inference. Below are five statements that may or may not be inferences based on information in the article. Label the statements using the following key:

C—Correct Inference   F—Faulty Inference

_____ 1. Doctors suspected that Patti White Bull was in danger of going into a coma even before she entered the hospital.

_____ 2. The human brain must have a steady supply of oxygen to work properly.

_____ 3. When a coma will end is difficult to predict.

_____ 4. Patti White Bull was angry when she found out that her husband had divorced her while she was in a coma.

_____ 5. Patti's coma would never have happened if doctors had been more careful.

Score 5 points for each correct answer.

_____ **Total Score:** Making Inferences

D | Using Words Precisely

Each numbered sentence below contains an underlined word or phrase from the article. Following the sentence are three definitions. One definition is closest to the meaning of the underlined word. One definition is opposite or nearly opposite. Label those two definitions using the following key; do not label the remaining definition.

C—Closest   O—Opposite or Nearly Opposite

1. She could not respond to the people around her. She was <u>unconscious</u>.

_____ a. not awake; dead to the world

_____ b. alert

_____ c. sleepy

2. In fact, she had been so <u>upbeat</u> that her nickname was Happi.

_____ a. depressed

_____ b. cheerful

_____ c. musical

3. Her eyes were open, but <u>vacant</u>.

_____ a. bloodshot

_____ b. filled with emotion

_____ c. empty and without expression

4. Still, it was <u>astounding</u> to see what she could do.

_____ a. astonishing or amazing

_____ b. joyful

_____ c. dull

5. Doctors expected her to spend the rest of her life in a <u>catatonic</u> state.

_____ a. extremely active

_____ b. without movement or expression

_____ c. sad

_____ Score 3 points for each correct C answer.

_____ Score 2 points for each correct O answer.

_____ **Total Score:** Using Words Precisely

Enter the four total scores in the spaces below, and add them together to find your Reading Comprehension Score. Then record your score on the graph on page 57.

Score	Question Type	Lesson 2
_____	Finding the Main Idea	
_____	Recalling Facts	
_____	Making Inferences	
_____	Using Words Precisely	
_____	**Reading Comprehension Score**	

Author's Approach

Put an X in the box next to the correct answer.

1. What is the authors' purpose in writing "Lost for 16 Years"?

☐ a. to inform the reader about what causes comas

☐ b. to describe a situation in which an unexplained medical miracle happened

☐ c. to emphasize the similarities between a coma and deep sleep

2. Which of the following statements from the article best describes Patti White Bull's condition between June 12, 1983, and late December 1999?

☐ a. She needed to learn many things all over again.

☐ b. In fact, she had been so upbeat that her nickname was Happi.

☐ c. She could not respond to the people around her. She was unconscious.

3. In this article, "It was hard for everyone to leave Patti behind" means that

☐ a. all the family members felt sad when they had to leave Patti in the nursing home and continue their lives.

☐ b. it was difficult to get Patti admitted into the nursing home.

☐ c. state laws made it difficult for family members to move away from New Mexico.

_____ Number of correct answers

Record your personal assessment of your work on the Critical Thinking Chart on page 58.

Summarizing and Paraphrasing

Follow the directions provided for questions 1 and 2. Put an X in the box next to the correct answer for question 3.

1. Complete the following one-sentence summary of the article using the lettered phrases from the phrase bank below. Write the letters on the lines.

Phrase Bank

a. how Patti White Bull fell into a coma

b. a description of Patti White Bull after she came out of the coma

c. a description of Patti White Bull entering the hospital

The article "Lost for 16 Years" begins with _____, goes on

to explain _____, and ends with _____.

2. Reread paragraph 19 in the article. Below, write a summary of the paragraph in no more than 25 words.

_____

_____

_____

_____

Reread your summary and decide whether it covers the important ideas in the paragraph. Next, decide how to shorten the summary to 15 words or less without leaving out any essential information. Write this summary below.

_____

_____

_____

3. Choose the best one-sentence paraphrase for the following sentence from the article: "There [Patti] remained locked in what doctors called a semi-vegetative state."

☐ a. Patti was trapped in a condition in which she couldn't react like a normal human being.

☐ b. Doctors required Patti to eat only vegetables.

☐ c. The doctors at the nursing home locked Patti in a room with many growing plants.

_____ Number of correct answers

Record your personal assessment of your work on the Critical Thinking Chart on page 58.

Critical Thinking

Put an X in the box next to the correct answer for questions 1 and 2. Follow the directions provided for the other questions.

1. Which of the following statements from the article is an opinion rather than a fact?

☐ a. Mark hoped Patti would come out of the coma quickly.

☐ b. After 16 years Patti White Bull had woken up.

☐ c. Once Patti woke up, doctors kept giving her amantadine.

CRITICAL THINKING

2. From what the article told about Patti's children's reaction to her current alert condition, you can predict that they will

☐ a. soon blame her for leaving them for so many years.

☐ b. continue to appreciate having their mother awake.

☐ c. soon begin to ignore their mother and live their own lives.

3. Choose from the letters below to correctly complete the following statement. Write the letters on the lines.

In the article, _____ and _____ are different.

a. Patti's condition after the birth of her first child

b. Patti's condition after the birth of her second child

c. Patti's condition after the birth of her fourth child

4. Choose from the letters below to correctly complete the following statement. Write the letters on the lines.

According to the article, _____ caused Patti White Bull to

_____, and the effect was _____.

a. stop breathing

b. no oxygen got to her brain for six minutes

c. a blood clot lodged in her lung

5. In which paragraph did you find your information or details to answer question 4? _____

_____ Number of correct answers

Record your personal assessment of your work on the Critical Thinking Chart on page 58.

Personal Response

If you could ask the authors of the article one question, what would it be?

_____

_____

_____

_____

Self-Assessment

A word or phrase in the article that I do not understand is _____

_____

_____

_____

_____

The Weird World of Howard Hughes

For 50 years, Howard Hughes lived the American dream. He set up businesses that made huge amounts of money. He designed airplanes that set new flying records. He dated movie stars and got to know famous politicians. But if Hughes's early years were a dream, his later years were a nightmare.

2   Howard Robard Hughes was born the day before Christmas in 1905. He

Howard Hughes designed and raced airplanes. He is pictured here at the controls of his Spruce Goose, *the largest plane ever built. This plane had eight engines and could seat 700 passengers—and it barely got off the ground.*

grew up in Texas. His father worked in the oil fields there. Young Howard did not like school. He dropped out at age 17. He did have a talent for math, though. And he liked to invent things. When his parents would not buy him a motorcycle, Hughes built his own. He also found a way to get his pilot's license. He used his allowance money to pay for flying lessons.

3 As a young man, Hughes used his talents to succeed in business. His father died in 1924 and left his share of the Hughes Tool Company to his son. Howard Hughes built the company into a $150-million business. At age 21, Hughes also began producing movies. He had his first hit, *Hell's Angels*, in 1930.

4 His golden touch didn't end there. In 1936 he took a chance on a new airline. The result was TWA, a $500-million company. Hughes designed an airplane called the H-1 racer. It flew across the country so fast it set a new speed record. Hughes bought some hotels in Las Vegas. As the casino business there grew, Hughes's fortune soared to more than $1 billion.

5 Every now and then, Hughes did have a failure. He suffered through several plane crashes. One almost killed him. He also saw the flop of his *Spruce Goose*. This was a plane Hughes designed. It was the biggest plane ever built. Measuring 320 feet long, it was 60% longer than a Boeing 747! Hughes managed to get the *Spruce Goose* in the air, but just barely. In a test run, it rose only 70 feet.

6 Despite these setbacks, Hughes was wildly successful. By the age of 45, he had it made. He was one of the richest men in the world. He could have lived in the greatest luxury. He could have had the finest meals, the nicest clothes, the best parties. But Howard Hughes didn't want any of that. Instead, he turned his back on the world. He became more and more secretive. Before long, he was living the life of a strange, sad hermit.

7 Hughes began to pull out of the public spotlight in the late 1940s. He was angry because some government leaders questioned his honesty. He was also weakened by his latest plane crash. So Hughes started to go out less. He trusted fewer and fewer people.

Soon he was spending all his time in a dark hotel room. He went for days without getting out of bed. He rang a bell to summon aides when he needed something. As Hughes lost touch with people, he also lost his grip on reality. He became a man obsessed.

8 His obsession centered on germs. Hughes became convinced that deadly germs were everywhere. He was terrified of getting them on his body. So he tried never to touch another person. He made his aides wear gloves. Hughes also refused to hold anything in his bare hands. He used a Kleenex tissue as "insulation."

9 Gordon Margulis was one of Hughes's aides. He is quoted in the book *Howard Hughes: The Hidden Years* by James Phelan. Said Margulis, "When you were going to bring [Hughes] a spoon, . . . the spoon handle had to be wrapped in Kleenex and Scotch-taped. Then you would take another piece of Kleenex to hold the Kleenex wrapping, so the wrapping wouldn't get contaminated. [Hughes] would lift the wrapped spoon off the piece of Kleenex."

10 Hughes's fear of germs spread to clothes. He couldn't stand to have

buttons, zippers, or snaps brush against his skin. In fact, he hated to wear clothes at all. Sometimes he put on a loose-fitting pair of underwear. But much of the time he simply went naked. Before he lay down, his bed had to be lined with paper towels.

11   Hughes couldn't stand air conditioning. He was sure it spread germs. Even on the hottest days, he wouldn't let his aides turn it on. In addition, Hughes would eat only certain foods. He felt he could trust the Campbell Soup Company. If Campbell's soup was heated to exactly the right temperature, he decided, it was safe to eat. And so for months, he ate nothing but Campbell's chicken soup. When he finally grew tired of it, he switched to vegetable soup.

12   Hughes needed glasses but refused to wear them. After all, they would have touched his skin. Instead, he used a magnifying glass. That he could hold in his hand—after covering his hand with a tissue, of course. As he got older, Hughes lost his hearing. But he wouldn't wear hearing aids, either.

13   Although Hughes was afraid of germs, he lived in filth. He went years without a haircut. It was reported that his fingernails grew so long they curled like corkscrews. His room was never dusted, never vacuumed.

14   Hughes had one more dirty little secret. By the late 1960s, he was a drug addict. For a while, he took pain pills and sleeping pills. Then he moved up to stronger drugs. He began injecting himself with what he called "medication." Hughes paid doctors to get the drugs for him. Once a doctor refused. Hughes flew into a rage, firing the man on the spot. Still, Hughes kept sending the doctor money. That kept him from going to the police or to the newspapers with his story.

15   By 1972 the drugs and the poor diet had taken their toll. Hughes's mind was fuzzy. He couldn't always remember what he wanted to say. He was also deathly thin. At six feet four inches tall, he should have weighed close to 200 pounds. Instead, Hughes weighed just 120 pounds.

16   That year, Hughes broke his leg while on the way to the shower. Although doctors set the bone, Hughes refused to walk again. According to one source, the doctors "pleaded with him, begged him, tried everything they could to get him to walk. He refused to budge."

17   And so, in the end, Howard Hughes even gave up the freedom to walk around his room. This man who had been such a success had turned into a prisoner in his own private prison. When he died in 1976, he was worth almost $2 billion. But only 16 people came to see him buried in an unmarked grave. Not one of them shed any tears. 🐉

If you have been timed while reading this article, enter your reading time below. Then turn to the Words-per-Minute Table on page 55 and look up your reading speed (words per minute). Enter your reading speed on the graph on page 56.

Reading Time: Lesson 3

_____ : _____
Minutes   Seconds

A Finding the Main Idea

One statement below expresses the main idea of the article. One statement is too general, or too broad. The other statement explains only part of the article; it is too narrow. Label the statements using the following key:

M—Main Idea   **B—Too Broad**   **N—Too Narrow**

_____ 1. Howard Hughes was unusually worried about the effects of germs.

_____ 2. Howard Hughes proved that money doesn't always bring happiness.

_____ 3. Billionaire Howard Hughes lived for many years as a strange, demanding hermit.

_____ Score 15 points for a correct M answer.

_____ Score 5 points for each correct B or N answer.

_____ **Total Score:** Finding the Main Idea

B Recalling Facts

How well do you remember the facts in the article? Put an X in the box next to the answer that correctly completes each statement about the article.

1. Howard Hughes's father worked
   ☐ a. in Texas oil fields.
   ☐ b. on a ranch in Oklahoma.
   ☐ c. in a factory in Arkansas.

2. One of Hughes's early successes was
   ☐ a. buying United Airlines.
   ☐ b. designing the H-1 racer airplane.
   ☐ c. flying faster than the speed of sound.

3. Hughes began to pull away from society in the
   ☐ a. late 1940s.
   ☐ b. late 1950s.
   ☐ c. 1960s.

4. Hughes would touch objects only if they were
   ☐ a. sprayed with alcohol
   ☐ b. first washed thoroughly.
   ☐ c. covered with Kleenex tissues.

5. Hughes said that the drugs he took were his
   ☐ a. medication.
   ☐ b. insulation.
   ☐ c. obsession.

Score 5 points for each correct answer.

_____ **Total Score:** Recalling Facts

C Making Inferences

When you combine your own experience and information from a text to draw a conclusion that is not directly stated in that text, you are making an inference. Below are five statements that may or may not be inferences based on information in the article. Label the statements using the following key:

C—Correct Inference   **F—Faulty Inference**

_____ 1. As a young man, Hughes was resourceful and daring.

_____ 2. During his final years, Howard Hughes prided himself on wearing the latest clothing styles.

_____ 3. Hughes's aides kept a large supply of Kleenex tissues on hand at all times.

_____ 4. Most people enjoyed visiting Howard Hughes in his hotel room.

_____ 5. The only people that Howard Hughes respected and obeyed were his doctors.

Score 5 points for each correct answer.

_____ **Total Score:** Making Inferences

D Using Words Precisely

Each numbered sentence below contains an underlined word or phrase from the article. Following the sentence are three definitions. One definition is closest to the meaning of the underlined word. One definition is opposite or nearly opposite. Label those two definitions using the following key; do not label the remaining definition.

C—Closest   **O—Opposite or Nearly Opposite**

1. Despite these setbacks, Hughes was wildly successful.

_____ a. co-workers

_____ b. victories

_____ c. disappointments or difficulties

2. Before long, he was living the life of a strange, sad hermit.

_____ a. one who lives away from other people

_____ b. one who loves nature

_____ c. one who lives with many other people

3. He rang a bell to summon aides when he needed something.

_____ a. send away

_____ b. call for

_____ c. scold

4. His obsession centered on germs.

_____ a. speech

_____ b. constant thoughts about a subject

_____ c. indifference

5. "Then you would take another piece of Kleenex to hold the Kleenex wrapping, so the wrapping wouldn't get <u>contaminated</u>."

_____ a. clean and pure

_____ b. wrinkled

_____ c. dirty; full of germs

_____ Score 3 points for each correct C answer.

_____ Score 2 points for each correct O answer.

_____ **Total Score:** Using Words Precisely

Enter the four total scores in the spaces below, and add them together to find your Reading Comprehension Score. Then record your score on the graph on page 57.

Score	Question Type	Lesson 3
_____	Finding the Main Idea	
_____	Recalling Facts	
_____	Making Inferences	
_____	Using Words Precisely	
_____	**Reading Comprehension Score**	

Author's Approach

Put an X in the box next to the correct answer.

1. What do the authors mean by the statement "But if Hughes's early years were a dream, his later years were a nightmare"?

☐ a. Although Hughes made a great deal of money in his youth, he lost it when he got older.

☐ b. As a young man, Hughes was happy and successful, but in his later years he became unhappy and strange.

☐ c. Hughes usually dreamed good dreams in his early years and bad dreams in his old age.

2. From the statements below, choose those that you believe the authors would agree with.

☐ a. Howard Hughes was hardworking and creative when he was young.

☐ b. Howard Hughes blamed his parents for not leaving him enough money.

☐ c. Howard Hughes lost most of his friends toward the end of his life.

3. Choose the statement below that best describes the authors' position in paragraph 17.

☐ a. Howard Hughes may have been rich, but he lost sight of what is most important in life.

☐ b. Howard Hughes was not likable.

☐ c. When rich people die, no one cares.

_____ Number of correct answers

Record your personal assessment of your work on the Critical Thinking Chart on page 58.

Summarizing and Paraphrasing

Follow the directions provided for questions 1 and 2. Put an X in the box next to the correct answer for question 3.

1. Complete the following one-sentence summary of the article using the lettered phrases from the phrase bank below. Write the letters on the lines.

> **Phrase Bank**
> a. how Hughes changed as he aged
> b. Hughes's early successes
> c. a description of Hughes in his final days

The article about Howard Hughes begins with _____, goes

on to explain _____, and ends with _____.

2. Reread paragraph 12 in the article. Below, write a summary of the paragraph in no more than 25 words.

_____

_____

_____

_____

Reread your summary and decide whether it covers the important ideas in the paragraph. Next, decide how to shorten the summary to 15 words or less without leaving out any essential information. Write this summary below.

_____

_____

_____

3. Choose the best one-sentence paraphrase for the following sentence from the article: "By 1972 the drugs and the poor diet had taken their toll."

☐ a. Even though Hughes observed a strict diet and used drugs from the doctor, he was still sick in 1972.

☐ b. In 1972 a toll was charged for using drugs and eating a poor diet.

☐ c. By 1972 it became clear that the combination of drug use and poor diet had been harmful.

> _____ Number of correct answers
>
> Record your personal assessment of your work on the Critical Thinking Chart on page 58.

Critical Thinking

Put an X in the box next to the correct answer for questions 1, 4, and 5. Follow the directions provided for the other questions.

1. Which of the following statements from the article is an opinion rather than a fact?

☐ a. For 50 years Howard Hughes lived the American dream.

☐ b. Young Howard did not like school.

☐ c. That year, Hughes broke his leg while on the way to the shower.

2. Choose from the letters below to correctly complete the following statement. Write the letters on the lines.

On the positive side, _____, but on the negative side

_____.

   a. Howard Hughes's father worked in the oil fields in Texas

   b. Howard Hughes withdrew from the world and obsessed over germs in his later years

   c. Howard Hughes seemed happy in his early years

3. Reread paragraph 7. Then choose from the letters below to correctly complete the following statement. Write the letters on the lines.

According to paragraph 7, _____ happened because

_____.

   a. Hughes was angry with the government and he was physically weak

   b. Hughes lived in a hotel room

   c. Hughes went out in public less and less

4. How is this article related to "Bizarre Endings"?

☐ a. It tells where Howard Hughes lived and what he did just before his death.

☐ b. It describes the strange and destructive habits that Howard Hughes fell into at the end of his life.

☐ c. It describes Howard Hughes's life and accomplishments, as well as his later years and his death.

5. What did you have to do to answer question 1?

☐ a. find an opinion (what someone thinks about something)

☐ b. find a purpose (why something is done)

☐ c. find a comparison (how things are the same)

_____ Number of correct answers

Record your personal assessment of your work on the Critical Thinking Chart on page 58.

Personal Response

This article is different from other articles about rich people I've read because _____

_____

Howard Hughes is unlike other rich people because _____

_____

_____

Self-Assessment

When reading the article, I was having trouble with _____

_____

_____

_____

The Mystery of the Mary Celeste

On December 4, 1872, a ship called the *Dei Gratia* was sailing off the coast of Portugal. Captain David Morehouse stood on the deck. As he looked across the sea, he saw a ship in the distance. Something seemed odd about that ship. It had almost no sails on its masts. It drifted slowly as it bobbed up and down in the water. Morehouse decided to sail closer for a better look. As he did, he

"Our vessel is in beautiful trim," wrote Captain Benjamin Briggs to his mother before setting sail on a trans-Atlantic voyage in 1872. What could have changed his vessel, the Mary Celeste, *into a ghost ship less than a month after leaving port?*

noticed something else. There seemed to be no one on board the ship.

2　　Now Morehouse was alarmed. He ordered three of his crew members to row a small boat over to the ship. He told them to board it and find out what was going on. As these men approached, they saw the ship's name written on her bow. It was the *Mary Celeste*. The men climbed aboard and called out loudly. No one answered. As Captain Morehouse had feared, the *Mary Celeste* was abandoned.

3　　Morehouse's men saw that the large sails of the ship had been ripped away by the wind. Only a couple of small sails still worked. Two of the hatch covers were open. As a result, the bottom of the ship had filled with $3\frac{1}{2}$ feet of water. Still, the ship was in pretty good shape. In the words of one crew member, it was "fit to go round the world." And it still carried six months' worth of food and plenty of drinking water.

4　　But where were the *Mary Celeste*'s captain and crew? It turned out that 10 people had been on board the ship. There had been the captain, Benjamin Briggs, and his wife, Sarah. With them had been their two-year-old daughter, Sophia. In addition, there had been seven crew members.

5　　Had something caused these people to leave the ship? Perhaps, Morehouse thought. After all, the *Mary Celeste*'s only lifeboat was gone. So, too, were some of the instruments used for navigation. But if everyone had abandoned the ship, they had done so in a great hurry. They left all their gear behind. They didn't take extra clothes, nor did they take little Sophia's toys. No one bothered to tie down the wheel that steered the ship. Captain Briggs didn't take his sword. He didn't take his log book, either.

6　　This log book contained a record of the ship's voyage. The last entry was dated November 25. At that time, there seemed to be no problem with the *Mary Celeste*. Everything was going as planned.

7　　What happened after that last entry was written? Why would people abandon a perfectly good ship? Why would they set off across the sea in an open lifeboat?

8　　A court later tried to answer those questions. But none of the usual reasons applied. The ship had not been attacked by pirates. There had been no wild storm that swept everyone overboard. The crew had not staged a mutiny against the captain. Any of those events would have left some sign of damage or struggle. But none was found.

9　　No, the known facts turned out to be rather dull. The *Mary Celeste* had sailed from New York City on November 7. Captain Briggs had not expected any trouble. Before sailing, he wrote to his mother. "Our vessel is in beautiful trim," he wrote. "I hope we shall have a fine passage."

10　　Clearly something had gone wrong. But if it was not pirates, a storm, or a mutiny, what was it? A few people pointed to Morehouse. They thought he had killed everyone on board the *Mary Celeste*. Morehouse did make money when he brought the abandoned ship back to port. Under the law, he got to keep part of its cargo. But there was no evidence that he had done anything wrong. In fact, Morehouse and Briggs had been close friends. They had dined together the night before the *Mary Celeste* set sail.

11   Other people dreamed up other explanations. Some guessed that those on board the *Mary Celeste* had eaten bad food. That drove them raving mad and they all jumped into the sea. Others thought a spaceship had come down from the sky. It had scooped everyone up. Some claimed that the 10 missing people had been carried off by a giant octopus. And then there was the idea that Captain Briggs had been plagued by an evil nightmare. It drove him insane. According to this theory, it caused him to kill his wife, child, and crew. Briggs dumped their bodies overboard. Then he plunged into the sea himself.

12   There is one explanation that sounds less crazy. The *Mary Celeste* had a cargo of alcohol. It was stored in oak barrels at the bottom of the ship. Perhaps fumes leaked through the barrels. Briggs might have feared that the fumes would cause an explosion.

He might have opened the two hatches to let the fumes out. Then, to be safe, he might have ordered everyone into the lifeboat.

13   If it happened this way, Briggs was not really abandoning ship. He would have been planning to return as soon as the fumes were gone. He might have tied a long rope from the lifeboat to the ship. That way he could pull the lifeboat back to the *Mary Celeste* when it was safe to do so. But what if the rope broke? That would have set the lifeboat adrift. Surely the crew would have rowed like mad after the *Mary Celeste*. But perhaps they simply hadn't been able to catch her.

14   Even this explanation has holes in it. It is hard to believe that an experienced sea captain would have panicked over a few fumes. It is hard to believe that Captain Briggs would have ordered everyone off the ship without taking better precautions. All we are

left with, then, is a mystery. Captain Briggs, Sarah, Sophia, and the seven crew members were never seen again. Their true fate remains a mystery of the sea.

If you have been timed while reading this article, enter your reading time below. Then turn to the Words-per-Minute Table on page 55 and look up your reading speed (words per minute). Enter your reading speed on the graph on page 56.

Reading Time: Lesson 4

——————— : ———————
Minutes   *Seconds*

A | Finding the Main Idea

One statement below expresses the main idea of the article. One statement is too general, or too broad. The other statement explains only part of the article; it is too narrow. Label the statements using the following key:

M—Main Idea   **B—Too Broad**   **N—Too Narrow**

_____ 1. When Captain Morehouse found the deserted *Mary Celeste*, it still carried six months' worth of food and plenty of drinking water.

_____ 2. The fate of the crew and passengers on the *Mary Celeste* has been a mystery since the deserted ship was found drifting in the Atlantic Ocean in 1872.

_____ 3. Of all the mysteries of the oceans, the case of the *Mary Celeste* is one of the most puzzling.

_____ Score 15 points for a correct M answer.

_____ Score 5 points for each correct B or N answer.

_____ **Total Score:** Finding the Main Idea

B | Recalling Facts

How well do you remember the facts in the article? Put an X in the box next to the answer that correctly completes each statement about the article.

1. Captain Morehouse decided to sail closer to the *Mary Celeste* when he saw that it
   ☐ a. was running out of water.
   ☐ b. was sinking.
   ☐ c. seemed deserted.

2. Some people think that leaking alcohol fumes
   ☐ a. made the captain fear an explosion.
   ☐ b. made the crew members drunk.
   ☐ c. caused the captain to lose his mind.

3. The only items that were clearly missing were
   ☐ a. Sophia's toys and the captain's sword.
   ☐ b. the captain's log and extra clothes.
   ☐ c. navigation instruments and the lifeboat.

4. Some people thought that Morehouse had killed everyone on board because he
   ☐ a. was angry with the *Mary Celeste's* captain.
   ☐ b. wanted to keep part of the ship's cargo.
   ☐ c. was raving mad.

5. The *Mary Celeste* had a cargo of
   ☐ a. alcohol.
   ☐ b. coal.
   ☐ c. tools and cloth.

Score 5 points for each correct answer.

_____ **Total Score:** Recalling Facts

C | Making Inferences

When you combine your own experience and information from a text to draw a conclusion that is not directly stated in that text, you are making an inference. Below are five statements that may or may not be inferences based on information in the article. Label the statements using the following key:

C—Correct Inference   **F—Faulty Inference**

_____ 1. The *Mary Celeste* had probably been sailing in the Pacific Ocean when everyone left the ship.

_____ 2. Captain Morehouse had pretty good eyesight.

_____ 3. The *Mary Celeste* would have sunk eventually if no one had found it.

_____ 4. Captain Morehouse had been following the *Mary Celeste* ever since it set sail.

_____ 5. An explosion is more likely to happen when fumes are held in an enclosed space than when they are released in an open area.

Score 5 points for each correct answer.

_____ **Total Score:** Making Inferences

D | Using Words Precisely

Each numbered sentence below contains an underlined word or phrase from the article. Following the sentence are three definitions. One definition is closest to the meaning of the underlined word. One definition is opposite or nearly opposite. Label those two definitions using the following key; do not label the remaining definition.

C—Closest   **O—Opposite or Nearly Opposite**

1. As Captain Morehouse had feared, the *Mary Celeste* was <u>abandoned</u>.

_____ a. sinking

_____ b. deserted

_____ c. full of people

2. The ship had not been <u>attacked</u> by pirates.

_____ a. set upon violently; stormed

_____ b. helped

_____ c. sailed

3. And then there was the idea that Captain Briggs had been <u>plagued</u> by an evil nightmare.

_____ a. comforted

_____ b. bothered greatly

_____ c. amused

4. That would have set the lifeboat <u>adrift</u>.

_____ a. moving toward a clear goal

_____ b. beyond the horizon

_____ c. floating without control

5. It is hard to believe that Captain Briggs would have ordered everyone off the ship without taking better <u>precautions</u>.

_____ a. careful actions taken to prevent harm

_____ b. medicine

_____ c. risky actions

_____ Score 3 points for each correct C answer.

_____ Score 2 points for each correct O answer.

_____ **Total Score:** Using Words Precisely

Enter the four total scores in the spaces below, and add them together to find your Reading Comprehension Score. Then record your score on the graph on page 57.

Score	Question Type	Lesson 4
_____	Finding the Main Idea	
_____	Recalling Facts	
_____	Making Inferences	
_____	Using Words Precisely	
_____	**Reading Comprehension Score**	

Author's Approach

Put an X in the box next to the correct answer.

1. The authors use the first sentence of the article to

☐ a. describe the setting of the story.

☐ b. tell about the captain who found the *Mary Celeste*.

☐ c. entertain the reader with an amusing story.

2. Which of the following statements from the article best describes reasons why Captain Morehouse was puzzled when he boarded the *Mary Celeste*?

☐ a. As he looked across the sea, he saw a ship in the distance.

☐ b. Two of the hatch covers were open. As a result, the bottom of the ship had filled with $3\frac{1}{2}$ feet of water.

☐ c. [The people who had been on the ship] left all their gear behind. They didn't take extra clothes, nor did they take little Sophia's toys.

3. Judging by statements from the article, "The Mystery of the *Mary Celeste*," you can conclude that the authors want the reader to think that

☐ a. the people on the *Mary Celeste* had been kidnapped by space aliens.

☐ b. the *Mary Celeste's* captain had abandoned ship because he was afraid of an explosion.

☐ c. Captain Morehouse probably had killed everyone aboard the *Mary Celeste* so he could steal its cargo.

_____ Number of correct answers

Record your personal assessment of your work on the Critical Thinking Chart on page 58.

Summarizing and Paraphrasing

Put an X in the box next to the correct answer.

1. Below are summaries of the article. Choose the summary that says all the most important things about the article, but in the fewest words.

☐ a. No one knows why the *Mary Celeste* was abandoned off Portugal's coast in 1872. There was no evidence of violence. People have created many theories about the fate of the ship's crew and passengers.

☐ b. When the *Mary Celeste* started its voyage in November 1872, the captain thought that the trip would be uneventful, but he was wrong.

☐ c. After Captain David Morehouse found the abandoned *Mary Celeste*, he searched for clues to explain the disappearance of the crew and the captain and his family. Some people believe that everyone on board was poisoned by bad food, while others think that an octopus carried them off or the captain went insane. We will never know what really happened.

2. Choose the sentence that correctly restates the following sentence from the article: "Morehouse's men saw that the large sails of the ship had been ripped away by the wind."

☐ a. The wind blew as Morehouse's men boarded the ship with torn sails.

☐ b. As Morehouse's men watched, the large sails of the ship were ripped away by the wind.

☐ c. Morehouse's men found that the wind had ripped the ship's sails.

_____ Number of correct answers

Record your personal assessment of your work on the Critical Thinking Chart on page 58.

Critical Thinking

Put an X in the box next to the correct answer for questions 1, 2, and 4. Follow the directions provided for the other questions.

1. Which of the following statements from the article is an opinion rather than a fact?

☐ a. The *Mary Celeste* had sailed from New York City on November 7.

☐ b. The last entry was dated November 25. At that time, there seemed to be no problem with the *Mary Celeste*.

☐ c. It is hard to believe that an experienced sea captain would have panicked over a few fumes.

2. Considering Captain Morehouse's actions as described in this article, you can predict that he would have

☐ a. tried hard to find Captain Briggs and his family.

☐ b. passed the *Mary Celeste* by if he hadn't known its captain personally.

☐ c. stolen all the cargo aboard the *Mary Celeste* if he had had the chance.

3. Choose from the letters below to correctly complete the following statement. Write the letters on the lines.

In the article, _____ and _____ are alike because both were lost at sea.

a. David Morehouse

b. Benjamin Briggs

c. Sarah Briggs

4. What was the first cause of Captain Morehouse's curiosity about the ship he saw in the distance?

☐ a. The captain could see that it was his friend's ship.

☐ b. The ship had almost no sails and it seemed to be drifting.

☐ c. The ship had no people aboard it.

5. In which paragraph did you find your information or details to answer question 4? _____

_____ Number of correct answers

Record your personal assessment of your work on the Critical Thinking Chart on page 58.

Personal Response

I agree with the author because _____

_____

_____

_____

_____

Self-Assessment

I'm proud of the way I answered question _____ in the _____ section because _____

_____

_____

_____

_____

"I Buried Paul"

The rain was coming down in sheets. The roads near London, England, were slick that early morning in 1966. Paul McCartney might have been driving too fast. Or perhaps he just didn't see a curve in the road. In any case, the singer lost control of his car. He crashed into a pole and died amid the flaming wreckage.

2   This was the grim story that spread in late 1969. At first, no one believed it. Paul McCartney could not be dead. No accident report had ever been

The Beatles were the hottest music act in the world during the 1960s and early 1970s. How could the death of one of them be kept a secret? Many fans believed the Abbey Road *album cover revealed evidence of Paul McCartney's death.*

filed. No death certificate had ever been issued. Besides, Paul was a member of the Beatles, the most famous rock group in the world. Fans saw him in concerts all the time. So of course he wasn't dead.

3   Or was he? According to the rumors, Paul had indeed died on a rainy road near London. His death had been kept a secret for three long years. The Beatles had covered up his fate because they didn't want their fans to know the truth. They feared it would hurt their popularity. And so, the story went, they hired a fake Paul to take the place of the real one. This second Paul looked, acted, and sang like the real thing. He played the guitar the same way and wrote the same kinds of songs. He was so good that he fooled everyone.

4   It is not clear how the rumors of Paul's death started. They might have begun with a Michigan student named Fred LaBour. He wrote an article for his college paper. In it, LaBour reviewed *Abbey Road*. This was the Beatles' latest album. LaBour claimed the album contained many clues that the real Paul was dead.

5   The rumors might have started at a radio station in Detroit. Three disc jockeys there were sure that Paul was dead. They passed their thoughts on to their listeners. Or perhaps the rumors came from a New York disc jockey named Roby Young. He, too, went on the air to say that Paul was dead.

6   It did not really matter how the rumors started. Once they began, they spread like wildfire. They were all that music fans could talk about for weeks. One radio station got more than 35,000 phone calls about Paul's death. Hundreds of mourners lined up in front of Paul's home in London. "The panic was unquenchable," said one writer.

7   So what was the "proof"? What convinced all these fans that Paul was dead? According to some people, clues were everywhere. All you had to do was look and listen. One piece of "evidence" was the *Abbey Road* album cover. It showed the four Beatles walking across a street called Abbey Road. That seemed normal enough. But a closer look revealed that Paul was out of step with the other three. He was the only one walking barefoot.

And he was holding a cigarette in the wrong hand. These things were seen as important messages. They were considered hints from the Beatles about the awful truth: Paul really was dead.

8   One fan made a truly wild claim. When Vaseline was smeared on the cover of *Abbey Road*, the fan said, the face of Paul just faded away. That claim seemed pretty far-fetched. Still, the album cover spooked many Beatles fans.

9   Then there was the photo on the cover of the album *Sgt. Pepper's Lonely Hearts Club Band*. It pictured Paul wearing an O.P.D. patch. Frightened fans knew the meaning of those initials. They stood for an English police term. It meant "Officially Pronounced Dead." Hmmm . . .

10   The most powerful clues came from the music itself. Fans became convinced that the Beatles' songs contained answers. They began to play the music faster or slower than usual. They taped many songs and then played them backward. By doing all this, they came up with several startling messages. One was John

Lennon saying, "Paul is dead. Miss him. Miss him. Miss him."

11 One song that was played backward was "Revolution No. 9." Heard in reverse, the song seemed to contain the sounds of a car crash. People thought they heard flames crackle. And they heard a voice cry, "Get me out! Get me out!" Another voice seemed to say, "He hit a pole! We better get him to a surgeon." Then came a scream, followed by a voice saying, "My wings are broken." Finally, many people heard these eerie words: "Turn me on, dead man."

12 The song "Strawberry Fields" also created a stir. At the very end of the song, John Lennon spoke a few garbled words. His voice was low and slow. It was hard to tell what he was saying. But after playing it again and again, most people thought they had it figured out. Lennon was saying, "I buried Paul."

13 "Strawberry Fields" also contained the sound of a sea gull. When speeded up, however, it sounded more like a man laughing. Was that Paul's voice? Was he laughing from the grave? It was a chilling thought.

14 As the clues piled up, more and more fans believed that Paul was dead. The Beatles, meanwhile, refused to comment on the rumors. Some people thought that proved the rumors were true. Others said the Beatles' silence was just a publicity move. After all, the rumors didn't exactly hurt record sales. In fact, sales during this time soared. Fans flocked to buy Beatles albums. They wanted to hear any hidden messages the records might contain.

15 In late 1969 the Beatles spoke up at last. Paul McCartney was not dead, their agent said. In fact, the agent called the rumors "a load of old rubbish." Some fans refused to believe him. They didn't change their minds when shown recent pictures of Paul. They simply thought the pictures showed the fake Paul. "They won't take 'no' for an answer when told that Paul's alive," grumbled the agent.

16 Finally, the real Paul McCartney spoke out. "I am alive and well," he said. That seemed to satisfy most fans. A few continued to believe he was dead. But most accepted the truth. They were relieved that their idol had *not* died. But questions remained. Why all the "messages" in Beatles songs and albums?

17 As it turned out, most were not messages at all. There was no special meaning to the *Abbey Road* cover or the *Sgt. Pepper* photo. And there were no messages in songs played backward or at different speeds. People had just let their imaginations run wild. John Lennon did say something at the end of the song "Strawberry Fields." But he didn't say "I buried Paul." All he really said was "cranberry sauce."

A Finding the Main Idea

One statement below expresses the main idea of the article. One statement is too general, or too broad. The other statement explains only part of the article; it is too narrow. Label the statements using the following key:

M—Main Idea   **B—Too Broad**   **N—Too Narrow**

_____ 1. Rumors that singer Paul McCartney had died spread wildly among fans in the late 1960s.

_____ 2. Fans "saw" clues about Paul McCartney's death in the photos on Beatles album covers.

_____ 3. Without any real evidence, many fans believed rumors about the famous rock group the Beatles.

_____ Score 15 points for a correct M answer.

_____ Score 5 points for each correct B or N answer.

_____ **Total Score:** Finding the Main Idea

B Recalling Facts

How well do you remember the facts in the article? Put an X in the box next to the answer that correctly completes each statement about the article.

1. According to the rumor, Paul died in a
☐ a. drug overdose.
☐ b. plane crash.
☐ c. car accident.

2. Fans found this clue suggesting Paul's death on the *Abbey Road* album cover: Paul
☐ a. was barefoot.
☐ b. was missing.
☐ c. looked too young.

3. Fans thought they heard John Lennon say "I buried Paul" at the end of
☐ a. *Sgt. Pepper's Lonely Hearts Club Band.*
☐ b. "Strawberry Fields."
☐ c. "Revolution No. 9."

4. At this time, Paul lived in
☐ a. Liverpool.
☐ b. Glasgow.
☐ c. London.

5. Most fans rejected the rumors when
☐ a. newspapers published Paul's picture.
☐ b. Paul himself said he was alive and well.
☐ c. Paul appeared in a concert.

Score 5 points for each correct answer.

_____ **Total Score:** Recalling Facts

C Making Inferences

When you combine your own experience and information from a text to draw a conclusion that is not directly stated in that text, you are making an inference. Below are five statements that may or may not be inferences based on information in the article. Label the statements using the following key:

C—Correct Inference   **F—Faulty Inference**

_____ 1. The technology of the 1960s included tape machines that could play a tape backward.

_____ 2. The Beatles were tremendously popular in both the United States and England.

_____ 3. From the beginning, the members of the Beatles were unhappy about the rumors of Paul's death.

_____ 4. Many people are able to convince themselves that just about any idea is true.

_____ 5. Some Beatles fans had plenty of extra time on their hands.

Score 5 points for each correct answer.

_____ **Total Score:** Making Inferences

D Using Words Precisely

Each numbered sentence below contains an underlined word or phrase from the article. Following the sentence are three definitions. One definition is closest to the meaning of the underlined word. One definition is opposite or nearly opposite. Label those two definitions using the following key; do not label the remaining definition.

C—Closest   **O—Opposite or Nearly Opposite**

1. The roads near London, England, were <u>slick</u> that early morning in 1966.

_____ a. dry

_____ b. winding

_____ c. slippery

2. This was the <u>grim</u> story that spread in late 1969.

_____ a. happy

_____ b. gloomy

_____ c. memorable

3. "The panic was <u>unquenchable</u>," said one writer.

_____ a. not able to be put out or stopped

_____ b. not able to be seen

_____ c. easily lessened

4. That claim seemed pretty <u>far-fetched</u>.

_____ a. distant

_____ b. unbelievable

_____ c. reasonable

5. They stood for an English police term. It meant "Officially Pronounced Dead."

_____ a. declared

_____ b. denied

_____ c. buried

_____ Score 3 points for each correct C answer.

_____ Score 2 points for each correct O answer.

_____ **Total Score:** Using Words Precisely

Enter the four total scores in the spaces below, and add them together to find your Reading Comprehension Score. Then record your score on the graph on page 57.

Score	Question Type	Lesson 5
_____	Finding the Main Idea	
_____	Recalling Facts	
_____	Making Inferences	
_____	Using Words Precisely	
_____	**Reading Comprehension Score**	

Author's Approach

Put an X in the box next to the correct answer.

1. The main purpose of the first paragraph is to

☐ a. emphasize how badly Paul McCartney drove his car.

☐ b. show how foolish fans can be.

☐ c. tell the rumor that shook the music world in 1969.

2. What is the authors' purpose in writing "I Buried Paul"?

☐ a. to encourage the reader to listen to Beatles songs

☐ b. to inform the reader about a strange rumor of Paul McCartney's death

☐ c. to express an opinion about rock music and its lyrics

3. From the statements below, choose those that you believe the authors would agree with.

☐ a. The Beatles themselves probably began the rumor of Paul's death.

☐ b. Some people bought Beatles albums just to see if the songs on them held messages about Paul's death.

☐ c. It is difficult to make out some of the words in Beatles songs.

4. In this article, "It did not really matter how the rumors started. Once they began, they spread like wildfire" means that

☐ a. once started, the rumors spread quickly and were difficult to stop.

☐ b. once the rumors started, they were easily put out, just as you put out a fire.

☐ c. like wildfires, the rumors were dangerous and destructive.

_____ Number of correct answers

Record your personal assessment of your work on the Critical Thinking Chart on page 58.

Summarizing and Paraphrasing

Follow the directions provided for questions 1 and 2. Put an X in the box next to the correct answer for question 3.

1. Complete the following one-sentence summary of the article using the lettered phrases from the phrase bank below. Write the letters on the lines.

> **Phrase Bank**
> a. McCartney's reassuring fans that he was still alive and the end of the panic
> b. how the rumor started and was spread
> c. a retelling of the rumor

The article about the rumor of Paul McCartney's death begins

with _____, goes on to explain _____, and ends with

_____.

2. Reread paragraph 4 in the article. Below, write a summary of the paragraph in no more than 25 words.

_____

_____

_____

Reread your summary and decide whether it covers the important ideas in the paragraph. Next, decide how to shorten the summary to 15 words or less without leaving out any essential information. Write this summary below.

_____

_____

_____

3. Read the statement from the article below. Then read the paraphrase of that statement. Choose the reason that best tells why the paraphrase does not say the same thing as the statement.

Statement: After studying the *Abbey Road* album cover, fans decided that Paul was dead because he was the only one who was barefoot in the photo.

Paraphrase: Fans who studied the *Abbey Road* album cover became convinced that Paul really was dead when they saw that he was out of step with the others, he was barefoot, and he was holding his cigarette in the wrong hand.

☐ a. Paraphrase says too much.

☐ b. Paraphrase doesn't say enough.

☐ c. Paraphrase doesn't agree with the statement.

> _____ Number of correct answers
>
> Record your personal assessment of your work on the Critical Thinking Chart on page 58.

Critical Thinking

Put an X in the box next to the correct answer for questions 1 and 4. Follow the directions provided for the other questions.

1. Which of the following statements from the article is an opinion rather than a fact?

☐ a. That claim seemed pretty far-fetched.

☐ b. One radio station got more than 35,000 phone calls about Paul's death.

☐ c. All he really said was "cranberry sauce."

2. Choose from the letters below to correctly complete the following statement. Write the letters on the lines.

On the positive side, _____, but on the negative side _____.

a. many fans mourned Paul's death unnecessarily

b. the rumor of Paul's death increased the sale of Beatles albums

c. the rumor may have been started by a student

3. Choose from the letters below to correctly complete the following statement. Write the letters on the lines.

According to the article, _____ caused Paul McCartney to _____, and the effect was that _____.

a. speak out to prove he was still alive

b. some fans were relieved that Paul was alive, but some still believed the rumor

c. the uproar about the rumor

4. Of the following theme categories, which would this story fit into?

☐ a. Celebrities sometimes try to fool the public.

☐ b. People who want to believe something badly enough can usually find evidence to prove it is true.

☐ c. Rock fans are more easily fooled than other people are.

_____ Number of correct answers

Record your personal assessment of your work on the Critical Thinking Chart on page 58.

Personal Response

I know how Paul McCartney felt when fans ignored what he had to say because _____

_____

_____

_____

_____

Before reading this article, I already knew _____

_____

_____

_____

_____

Compare and Contrast

Think about the articles you have read in Unit One. Pick the three articles that feature especially interesting people. Write the titles of the articles that tell about them in the first column of the chart below. Use information you learned from the articles to fill in the empy boxes in the chart.

Title	Name the interesting people involved in the story.	What did these people do that was interesting or strange?	Did you like or dislike the people involved in the story? Why?

The character I found most interesting was _____ I chose that person because _____

_____

_____

Words-per-Minute Table

Unit One

Directions: If you were timed while reading an article, refer to the Reading Time you recorded in the box at the end of the article. Use this words-per-minute table to determine your reading speed for that article. Then plot your reading speed on the graph on page 56.

Lesson / No. of Words	Sample 657	1 1,097	2 1,075	3 1,116	4 993	5 1,106	Seconds
1:30	438	731	717	744	662	737	**90**
1:40	394	658	645	670	596	664	**100**
1:50	358	598	586	609	542	603	**110**
2:00	329	549	538	558	497	553	**120**
2:10	303	506	496	515	458	510	**130**
2:20	282	470	461	478	426	474	**140**
2:30	263	439	430	446	397	442	**150**
2:40	246	411	403	419	372	415	**160**
2:50	232	387	379	394	350	390	**170**
3:00	219	366	358	372	331	369	**180**
3:10	207	346	339	352	314	349	**190**
3:20	197	329	323	335	298	332	**200**
3:30	188	313	307	319	284	316	**210**
3:40	179	299	293	304	271	302	**220**
3:50	171	286	280	291	259	289	**230**
4:00	164	274	269	279	248	277	**240**
4:10	158	263	258	268	238	265	**250**
4:20	152	253	248	258	229	255	**260**
4:30	146	244	239	248	221	246	**270**
4:40	141	235	230	239	213	237	**280**
4:50	136	227	222	231	205	229	**290**
5:00	131	219	215	223	199	221	**300**
5:10	127	212	208	216	192	214	**310**
5:20	123	206	202	209	186	207	**320**
5:30	119	199	195	744	181	201	**330**
5:40	116	194	190	197	175	195	**340**
5:50	113	188	184	191	170	190	**350**
6:00	110	183	179	186	166	184	**360**
6:10	107	178	174	181	161	179	**370**
6:20	104	173	170	670	157	175	**380**
6:30	101	169	165	172	153	170	**390**
6:40	99	165	161	167	149	166	**400**
6:50	96	161	157	163	145	162	**410**
7:00	94	157	154	159	142	158	**420**
7:10	92	153	150	156	139	154	**430**
7:20	90	150	147	152	135	151	**440**
7:30	88	146	143	149	132	147	**450**
7:40	86	143	140	146	130	144	**460**
7:50	84	140	137	142	127	141	**470**
8:00	82	137	134	140	124	138	**480**

Minutes and Seconds

Plotting Your Progress: Reading Speed

Unit One

Directions: If you were timed while reading an article, write your words-per-minute rate for that article in the box under the number of the lesson. Then plot your reading speed on the graph by putting a small X on the line directly above the number of the lesson, across from the number of words per minute you read. As you mark your speed for each lesson, graph your progress by drawing a line to connect the X's.

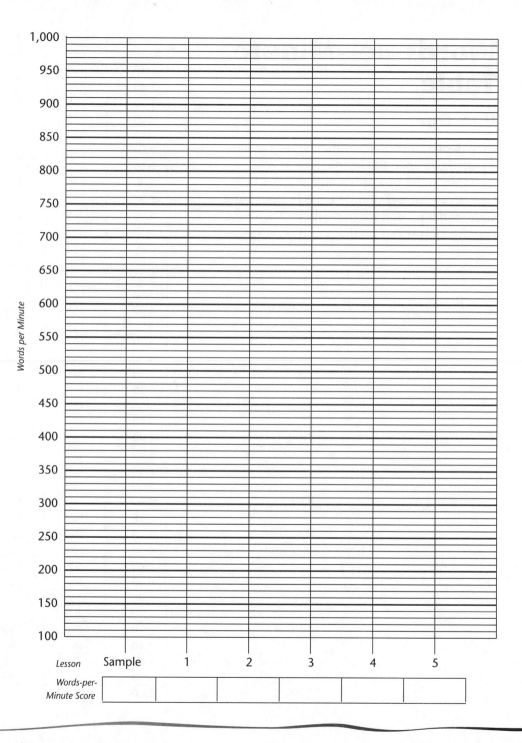

Lesson	Sample	1	2	3	4	5
Words-per-Minute Score						

Plotting Your Progress: Reading Comprehension

Unit One

Directions: Write your Reading Comprehension score for each lesson in the box under the number of the lesson. Then plot your score on the graph by putting a small X on the line directly above the number of the lesson and across from the score you earned. As you mark your score for each lesson, graph your progress by drawing a line to connect the X's.

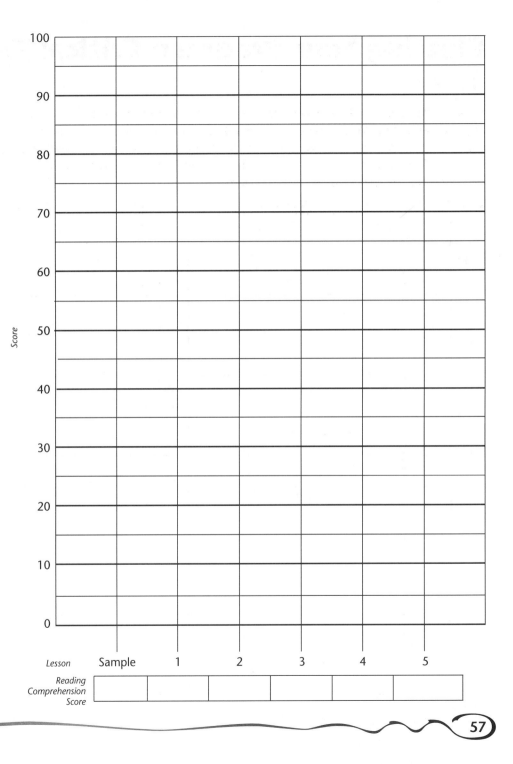

Plotting Your Progress: Critical Thinking

Unit One

Directions: Work with your teacher to evaluate your responses to the Critical Thinking questions for each lesson. Then fill in the appropriate spaces in the chart below. For each lesson and each type of Critical Thinking question, do the following: Mark a minus sign (–) in the box to indicate areas in which you feel you could improve. Mark a plus sign (+) to indicate areas in which you feel you did well. Mark a minus-slash-plus sign (–/+) to indicate areas in which you had mixed success. Then write any comments you have about your performance, including ideas for improvement.

Lesson	Author's Approach	Summarizing and Paraphrasing	Critical Thinking
Sample			
1			
2			
3			
4			
5			

UNIT TWO

The Lost Colony of Roanoke

John White was a leader of England's first colonists in America, who settled in North Carolina on an island called Roanoke. When White returned from England with supplies, he discovered that the colonists had vanished. The word CROATOAN is the only clue they left.

John White stood on the ship's deck. He peered across the water toward the little island of Roanoke. It had been three long years since he had left this island. Now, at last, he was coming back.

2   White was excited. He couldn't wait to see his daughter, Eleanor. Surely she would have much to tell him about life on Roanoke. And his little granddaughter, Virginia Dare, would be three years old now. The last time White had seen her she was just an infant. White had a special place in his heart for this child. She was the first English child born in the New World.

3   The captain anchored the ship off the Outer Banks of what is now North Carolina. White watched smoke rise from Roanoke Island. He assumed it was coming from the settlement where his daughter and 120 other English colonists lived. Someone must have started a cooking fire.

4   It was getting late in the day. Still, White wanted to row over to the island. He was looking forward to a happy reunion with the colonists. After all, White himself had helped start this settlement. He was its governor. He and the others had moved here from England in 1587. White had left to get more supplies from England. It had taken a long time, but he had done it. Now he was eager to rejoin his family on Roanoke Island.

5   And so, on August 15, 1590, White and some shipmates rowed to the island. White did not want the colonists to think they were being attacked. He wanted them to know it was a friendly group that was arriving. So he asked one man to blow on a trumpet. Then White and his shipmates began to sing. They belted out one old folk song after another as they walked toward the settlement.

6   But when they arrived, White looked around in shock. The place was deserted. There was not a colonist in sight. White couldn't believe it. The colonists had to be here. They just had to be! After all, he had seen smoke curling up from their cooking fires. But there was no sign of them now.

7   Taking a closer look around, White saw that many of the homes had been torn down. A fence had been erected around the area. It looked as though it had served as a kind of fort. But White found no dead bodies, no sign of a struggle. He saw that many of the colonists' possessions were still around. Lots of things had been neatly buried. White uncovered books, pictures, and his old suit of armor.

8   Reluctantly, White faced the truth. His daughter and the others were not here. The smoke he had seen must have been coming from a fire started by lightning. It appeared that the colonists had abandoned the settlement some time ago.

9   But why? If they had fled from danger, they would not have had time to hide their things. If they had not been in danger, why had they fled? And why had they left no message?

10   A message! That was it! White recalled a system they had set up

before he left. If for any reason the colonists moved to a new place, they agreed to carve its name on a nearby tree. If they were in trouble, they would carve a cross next to the name. White did find the letters *C R O* carved in a tree. He also found the word *CROATOAN* carved on a post in the fence. Neither carving showed a cross.

11　Croatoan. This was the name of another island (one that is now known as Hatteras). It was also the home of Manteo, an Indian who had been helping the colonists. It made sense that the colonists would turn to Manteo's people in time of need. Perhaps the colonists had chosen to move to that island. Or perhaps they had been driven there by some hostile group. In any case, White felt hope rise in his chest. He thought he might find Eleanor, Virginia, and the others safely settled on Croatoan Island.

12　White asked the captain of the ship to take him to Croatoan. At first the captain seemed willing. But a storm came up, delaying the trip. Then the captain began to worry about food and water supplies. He wanted to move on to the West Indies without further delay. White tried to get him to change his mind, but it was no use. John White knew he could not stay in the wilderness alone. And so when the ship sailed for the West Indies, White was on it. He

never got to look around Croatoan or any other nearby region. All he could do was hope that the colonists—wherever they might be—were safe and well.

13　Over the next 13 years, five different ships did go in search of the "lost colonists." But no one ever found them. They had vanished. Historians have come up with several theories about what happened. According to one, the colonists got tired of waiting for John White to come back with supplies. They built their own ship and tried to sail across the Atlantic. They did not make it. The ship and the colonists were swallowed up by the sea. This might have happened. But why didn't the colonists leave a message on Roanoke explaining their plans?

14　Another theory is that the colonists were killed by hostile Indians. It is true that the colonists had angered local Roanoke Indians. But if these Indians killed them, why were no bodies ever found? Why was there no sign of a struggle at the settlement?

15　One theory maintains that the colonists moved off the island by choice. The soil on Roanoke Island was not very good for farming. So the colonists went looking for better land to the west. They settled down near the Chesapeake Indians. They were killed when the Chesapeakes were wiped out by a rival tribe. But if this happened,

why did the colonists carve the word CROATOAN on a post? Did some of the colonists go to Croatoan to wait for White? If so, what happened to them? Why were they never found?

16　One legend holds that the colonists did not die. Instead, they slowly blended into local Indian tribes. There are a couple of strange facts that seem to support this story. A hundred years after the colonists were lost, a man in Virginia reported an odd thing. He said he saw an Indian boy whose hair was "a perfect yellow." And in North Carolina, about two hundred miles from Roanoke, a group of blue-eyed Indians was found. These Lumbee Indians had some interesting last names. These included 41 names of the missing colonists.

If you have been timed while reading this article, enter your reading time below. Then turn to the Words-per-Minute Table on page 101 and look up your reading speed (words per minute). Enter your reading speed on the graph on page 102.

Reading Time: Lesson 6

_____ : _____
Minutes　　*Seconds*

A Finding the Main Idea

One statement below expresses the main idea of the article. One statement is too general, or too broad. The other statement explains only part of the article; it is too narrow. Label the statements using the following key:

M—Main Idea   B—Too Broad   N—Too Narrow

_____ 1. The mystery of the Roanoke colony is one that has puzzled historians for years.

_____ 2. One theory of the colonists' disappearance is that they moved west, seeking better farmland.

_____ 3. The people of the Roanoke colony simply vanished, leaving history with a fascinating mystery.

_____ Score 15 points for a correct M answer.

_____ Score 5 points for each correct B or N answer.

_____ **Total Score:** Finding the Main Idea

B Recalling Facts

How well do you remember the facts in the article? Put an X in the box next to the answer that correctly completes each statement about the article.

1. Virginia Dare was John White's
   ☐ a. daughter.
   ☐ b. granddaughter.
   ☐ c. wife.

2. As White approached Roanoke, he
   ☐ a. sang folk songs.
   ☐ b. beat on a drum.
   ☐ c. shot his gun into the air.

3. The word found carved into a fence post was
   ☐ a. *CHESAPEAKE.*
   ☐ b. *CROATOAN.*
   ☐ c. *HATTERAS.*

4. If the colonists were in trouble, they agreed to carve this on a tree by their destination's name:
   ☐ a. a skull and crossbones.
   ☐ b. SOS.
   ☐ c. a cross.

5. The captain of White's ship refused to sail to Croatoan Island because he
   ☐ a. wasn't sure where Croatoan Island was.
   ☐ b. was worried about food and supplies.
   ☐ c. wanted to get right back to England.

Score 5 points for each correct answer.

_____ **Total Score:** Recalling Facts

C Making Inferences

When you combine your own experience and information from a text to draw a conclusion that is not directly stated in that text, you are making an inference. Below are five statements that may or may not be inferences based on information in the article. Label the statements using the following key:

C—Correct Inference   **F—Faulty Inference**

_____ 1. Early American colonies were usually nervous about enemy attacks.

_____ 2. Wood was readily available on Roanoke Island.

_____ 3. Whoever carved CRO into a tree stopped because he or she didn't know how to spell the word.

_____ 4. The captain of White's return ship was probably a close family friend.

_____ 5. There was perfect peace among the tribes in America before Europeans settled there.

Score 5 points for each correct answer.

_____ **Total Score:** Making Inferences

D Using Words Precisely

Each numbered sentence below contains an underlined word or phrase from the article. Following the sentence are three definitions. One definition is closest to the meaning of the underlined word. One definition is opposite or nearly opposite. Label those two definitions using the following key; do not label the remaining definition.

C—Closest   **O—Opposite or Nearly Opposite**

1. He was looking forward to a happy <u>reunion with</u> the colonists.

   _____ a. separation from

   _____ b. rejoining with

   _____ c. dinner with

2. They <u>belted out</u> one old folk song after another as they walked toward the settlement.

   _____ a. remembered

   _____ b. sang loudly

   _____ c. sang softly

3. A fence had been <u>erected</u> around the area.

   _____ a. built

   _____ b. planned

   _____ c. torn down

4. Or perhaps they had been driven there by some <u>hostile</u> group.

   _____ a. local

   _____ b. unfriendly

   _____ c. friendly

5. They were killed when the Chesapeakes were wiped out by a <u>rival</u> tribe.

_____ a. cooperating

_____ b. strong

_____ c. competing

_____ Score 3 points for each correct C answer.

_____ Score 2 points for each correct O answer.

_____ **Total Score:** Using Words Precisely

Enter the four total scores in the spaces below, and add them together to find your Reading Comprehension Score. Then record your score on the graph on page 103.

Score	Question Type	Lesson 6
_____	Finding the Main Idea	
_____	Recalling Facts	
_____	Making Inferences	
_____	Using Words Precisely	
_____	**Reading Comprehension Score**	

Author's Approach

Put an X in the box next to the correct answer.

1. What is the authors' purpose in writing "The Lost Colony of Roanoke"?

□ a. to describe a situation in which colonists were wiped out because of the indifference of their governor

□ b. to inform the reader about a fascinating historical mystery

□ c. to instill in the reader a reverence for the past

2. Which of the following statements from the article best describes what John White saw when he first walked into Roanoke after his long trip?

□ a. He also found the word CROATOAN carved on a post in the fence.

□ b. A fence had been erected around the area.

□ c. The place was deserted.

3. From the statements below, choose those that you believe the authors would agree with.

□ a. The colonists probably slowly blended into local tribes.

□ b. The colonists were massacred in their homes by local tribes.

□ c. The word CROATOAN means nothing; it was just a decoration.

4. What do the authors imply by saying "He said he saw an Indian boy whose hair was 'a perfect yellow'"?

□ a. The boy must have come from England.

□ b. One of the Roanoke colonists could have been the boy's ancestor.

□ c. The tribe had probably taken the boy from an English family.

_____ Number of correct answers

Record your personal assessment of your work on the Critical Thinking Chart on page 104.

Summarizing and Paraphrasing

Follow the directions provided for question 1. Put an X in the box next to the correct answer for the other questions.

1. Look for the important ideas and events in paragraphs 6 and 7. Summarize those paragraphs in one or two sentences.

_____

_____

_____

_____

2. Below are summaries of the article. Choose the summary that says all the most important things about the article but in the fewest words.

☐ a. Ever since John White returned to Roanoke in 1590 to find the colony deserted, people have been wondering why it was abandoned and what happened to the colonists. Several theories have been suggested, but no single theory is accepted by all.

☐ b. John White was disappointed not to find his daughter and granddaughter in the colony of Roanoke when he returned there after a long voyage to England for supplies.

☐ c. One theory about the lost colony of Roanoke is that the people there built a ship and died while sailing back to England. Another theory is that a local tribe wiped them out. But both of those theories present problems.

3. Choose the best one-sentence paraphrase for the following sentence from the article: "If for any reason the colonists moved to a new place, they agreed to carve its name on a nearby tree."

☐ a. The colonists agreed to move to a place near an unusual tree.

☐ b. The colonists agreed that if they needed to move, they would carve the name of the place where they were going into a nearby tree.

☐ c. When they saw its name on a nearby tree, the colonists would agree to move to a new place.

> _____ Number of correct answers
>
> Record your personal assessment of your work on the Critical Thinking Chart on page 104.

Critical Thinking

Follow the directions provided for questions 1, 3, and 5. Put an X in the box next to the correct answer for the other questions.

1. For each statement below, write _O_ if it expresses an opinion or write _F_ if it expresses a fact.

_____ a. John White returned to England for more supplies.

_____ b. John White should have insisted that the captain go to Croatoan and help him look for the lost colonists.

_____ c. The island of Croatoan is now known as Hatteras.

2. From what the article told about the theories about the lost colony of Roanoke, you can predict that

☐ a. very soon, people will get bored with the question of what happened to the colonists at Roanoke and will stop thinking about it.

☐ b. everyone will eventually agree that the colonists moved in with the Chesapeake Indians and were wiped out in an attack on the Chesapeakes.

☐ c. people will keep wondering about this mystery for many years.

3. Choose from the letters below to correctly complete the following statement. Write the letters on the lines.

In the article, _____ and _____ are different.

a. the name of another island near Roanoke

b. the name of John White's granddaughter

c. the name written on the fence post

4. How is "The Lost Colony of Roanoke" an example of a bizarre ending?

☐ a. It is strange that the colony and all its residents simply disappeared without a trace.

☐ b. No one knows why the colonists built a fence around their settlement.

☐ c. No one knows why John White didn't search the island of Croatoan for his family.

5. Which paragraphs from the article provide evidence that supports your answer to question 3? _____

_____ Number of correct answers

Record your personal assessment of your work on the Critical Thinking Chart on page 104.

Personal Response

What do you think happened to the colonists of Roanoke? Explain. _____

_____

_____

_____

_____

Self-Assessment

Before reading this article, I already knew _____

_____

_____

_____

_____

The Strange Case of Mr. Wright

It was clear that the man was dying. Cancer had spread throughout his body. He had tumors the size of oranges in his neck and more tumors in his chest and groin. His lungs were filling up with milky fluid. To help him breathe, doctors had given him oxygen. But beyond that, there was not much they could do. They all knew he would be dead in a couple of weeks anyway.

Modern medicine depends on high-tech tools, the latest drugs, and expensive machinery and treatments. None of these, however, could give Mr. Wright back his health. What made him feel so much better?

2   The patient, known as "Mr. Wright," knew how bad things looked. Still, he believed he had one chance at survival. He wanted to try a brand new drug. It was called Krebiozen. The drug was being tested by doctors around the country. Already newspapers were calling it a wonder drug.

3   Mr. Wright asked his doctor, Philip West, if he could try some. Dr. West was skeptical. For one thing, the hospital did not have a big supply of the drug. West did not want to waste it. He was supposed to use it only on patients who were expected to live three months or longer. Mr. Wright did not meet that standard. Still, Mr. Wright pleaded for a chance. "As much as I tried to dissuade him, he begged . . . for this 'golden opportunity,'" Dr. West said later. "Against my better judgment, and against the rules of the Krebiozen committee, I decided I would have to [give the drug to] him."

4   And so, that Friday, Dr. West gave Mr. Wright a shot of the new drug. The doctor scheduled him for three more shots the following week. On Monday, Dr. West went to check on his patient.

He half-expected to find that the poor man had died over the weekend. From Dr. West's point of view, that would not have been the worst thing in the world. At least then the man's suffering would have ended. Then, too, Dr. West could give Mr. Wright's unused doses of Krebiozen to some other cancer victim.

5   But Philip West was in for a surprise. On Friday, Mr. Wright had been too weak to get out of bed. He had burned with fever. Every breath had been a struggle. Now West saw this same man walking cheerfully down the corridor. He looked happier and healthier than he had in months. When West examined him, he found the tumors had shrunk to half their original size. As West put it, "the tumor masses had melted like snowballs on a hot stove."

6   Dr. West was thrilled. The Krebiozen really worked! He hurried to see the 11 other patients who had received shots of it. But here was the bewildering part. None of the other patients showed the slightest improvement. In fact, a couple had gotten worse.

7   What was going on here? No one was sure. But 10 days after starting his Krebiozen shots, Mr. Wright left the hospital. "Practically all signs of his disease [had] vanished in this short time," said West.

8   Continuing his shots of Krebiozen, Mr. Wright stayed healthy for weeks. Then he began to read some disturbing news articles. The press reported that Krebiozen didn't work. Doctor after doctor claimed no success with it. Mr. Wright was crushed. He had believed in Krebiozen. He had trusted its power. And he thought it had cured him. Now doctors seemed to be saying it was worthless. Deeply discouraged, Mr. Wright fell ill again. Within days, his tumors reappeared. They quickly grew back to their full size. And so, once again, Mr. Wright lay at the edge of death.

9   By this time, Dr. West had a hunch. He suspected that Mr. Wright's cancer had not reacted to the drug. Instead, he thought the cure might have come from Mr. Wright's mental state. To this day, no one is sure how closely connected the mind and body really are. In the mid-1950s, when Mr.

Wright was fighting for his life, few people thought about that link. Still, Dr. West decided to explore it. He felt there was only one way for him to do it. He would have to lie.

10   West told Mr. Wright that the reports in the papers were incomplete. He claimed Krebiozen *did* work. However, the drug did not work well after it had been stored for any length of time. Dr. West said that was why other patients didn't respond to it. He also said that explained Mr. Wright's relapse. But, announced the doctor, the problem had been solved. Fresh Krebiozen—twice as strong as the first shipment—was on its way to the hospital. In just a day or two, Mr. Wright could begin a new series of shots with the fresh drug.

11   None of this was true, and today no doctor would be allowed to tell such lies. Still, Dr. West was doing what he thought was best for his patient. His "news" delighted Mr. Wright. The sick man regained his hope. He waited eagerly for the phantom shipment of Krebiozen.

12   After a couple of days, Dr. West told Mr. Wright that the drug had arrived. Then, "with much fanfare, and putting on quite an act," he gave his patient a shot "of the doubly potent, *fresh* [drug]." In truth, the shot contained nothing but fresh water. But Mr. Wright didn't know that. He was sure he was getting a lifesaving treatment.

13   Again, the tumors disappeared as if by magic. After a few shots, Mr. Wright bounced out of bed. His life returned to normal. He even went back to flying his own plane.

14   In the weeks after this second recovery, Mr. Wright checked the papers often. He was looking for news about Krebiozen. He wanted to know if other patients had responded to the fresh version of it. Two months passed. Mr. Wright saw no articles. Then he learned the truth. Doctors announced they were giving up on Krebiozen. The drug did nothing to help cancer patients.

15   For Mr. Wright this news was a death sentence. Again the cancer flared up. Dr. West sadly described the results. "Within a few days of this report, Mr. Wright was readmitted to the hospital. His faith was now gone, his last hope vanished, and he [died] in less than two days."

If you have been timed while reading this article, enter your reading time below. Then turn to the Words-per-Minute Table on page 101 and look up your reading speed (words per minute). Enter your reading speed on the graph on page 102.

Reading Time: Lesson 7

_____ : _____
Minutes   Seconds

A | Finding the Main Idea

One statement below expresses the main idea of the article. One statement is too general, or too broad. The other statement explains only part of the article; it is too narrow. Label the statements using the following key:

M—Main Idea   B—Too Broad   N—Too Narrow

_____ 1. The sudden but temporary recovery of a cancer patient, Mr. Wright, shows the power of the mind in affecting the body's healing powers.

_____ 2. Mr. Wright had heard of a new drug, Krebiozen, and desperately wanted to take it.

_____ 3. The role of the mind in affecting how the body reacts to illness is a subject of great interest to scientists and patients.

_____ Score 15 points for a correct M answer.

_____ Score 5 points for each correct B or N answer.

_____ **Total Score:** Finding the Main Idea

B | Recalling Facts

How well do you remember the facts in the article? Put an X in the box next to the answer that correctly completes each statement about the article.

1. Mr. Wright's doctors expected that his cancer would kill him
   ☐ a. in less than two weeks.
   ☐ b. within six months.
   ☐ c. within two years.

2. Days after his first shot of Krebiozen, Wright
   ☐ a. was well enough to leave his bed.
   ☐ b. was well enough to leave the hospital.
   ☐ c. showed little improvement.

3. Mr. Wright's health worsened when he
   ☐ a. stopped taking Krebiozen.
   ☐ b. left the hospital.
   ☐ c. thought that Krebiozen was worthless.

4. Dr. West suspected that Wright's improvement
   ☐ a. was due to the drug Krebiozen.
   ☐ b. was due to his faith in Krebiozen.
   ☐ c. would have occurred under any conditions.

5. Mr. Wright died because he had
   ☐ a. been given water instead of Krebiozen.
   ☐ b. lost faith in his treatment.
   ☐ c. a bad reaction to Krebiozen.

Score 5 points for each correct answer.

_____ **Total Score:** Recalling Facts

C | Making Inferences

When you combine your own experience and information from a text to draw a conclusion that is not directly stated in that text, you are making an inference. Below are five statements that may or may not be inferences based on information in the article. Label the statements using the following key:

C—Correct Inference   **F—Faulty Inference**

_____ 1. In at least some cases, what people believe about their health care is more important to their well-being than the care itself.

_____ 2. Doctors should lie to a patient whenever they think that lies will improve the patient's attitude.

_____ 3. Newspaper articles that highly praise a drug before the drug has been fully tested can lead patients to demand drugs that are worthless to them.

_____ 4. Patients should have complete control over their own treatment because then they will have more confidence in it and a better chance of getting well.

_____ 5. The case of Mr. Wright is one of a kind and therefore of no concern to doctors in general.

Score 5 points for each correct answer.

_____ **Total Score:** Making Inferences

D | Using Words Precisely

Each numbered sentence below contains an underlined word or phrase from the article. Following the sentence are three definitions. One definition is closest to the meaning of the underlined word. One definition is opposite or nearly opposite. Label those two definitions using the following key; do not label the remaining definition.

C—Closest   **O—Opposite or Nearly Opposite**

1. Mr. Wright asked his doctor, Philip West, if he could try some. Dr. West was <u>skeptical</u>.

_____ a. doubtful

_____ b. helpless

_____ c. confident; positive

2. "As much as I tried to <u>dissuade</u> him, he begged . . . for this 'golden opportunity,'" Dr. West said later.

_____ a. instruct

_____ b. persuade

_____ c. discourage

3. Dr. West said that was why other patients didn't <u>respond to</u> it.

_____ a. change for the better because of

_____ b. experience a bad reaction, or any reaction at all, to

_____ c. appreciate

4. He also said that explained Mr. Wright's <u>relapse</u>.

_____ a. improvement

_____ b. fit of laughter

_____ c. return to an earlier, sicklier condition

5. He waited eagerly for the <u>phantom</u> shipment of Krebiozen.

_____ a. late

_____ b. imaginary

_____ c. real; actual

_____ Score 3 points for each correct C answer.

_____ Score 2 points for each correct O answer.

_____ **Total Score:** Using Words Precisely

Enter the four total scores in the spaces below, and add them together to find your Reading Comprehension Score. Then record your score on the graph on page 103.

Score	Question Type	Lesson 7
_____	Finding the Main Idea	
_____	Recalling Facts	
_____	Making Inferences	
_____	Using Words Precisely	
_____	**Reading Comprehension Score**	

Author's Approach

Put an X in the box next to the correct answer.

1. The main purpose of the first paragraph is to

☐ a. explain how cancer kills its victims.

☐ b. describe Mr. Wright's physical condition.

☐ c. explain how doctors treat cancer.

2. Which of the following statements from the article best describes Mr. Wright's condition before he was given Krebiozen?

☐ a. Deeply discouraged, Mr. Wright fell ill again.

☐ b. He looked happier and healthier than he had in months.

☐ c. It was clear that the man was dying.

3. From the statements below, choose those that you believe the authors would agree with.

☐ a. The mind and the body work together closely.

☐ b. If a medicine works well with one victim of a disease, it will work with all patients with the same disease.

☐ c. Mr. Wright's health depended upon his faith in Krebiozen.

4. What do the authors imply by saying "For Mr. Wright this news was a death sentence"?

☐ a. When Mr. Wright heard the news, his body allowed the cancer to return and kill him.

☐ b. Mr. Wright was so angry when he heard the news that he decided to commit suicide.

☐ c. Mr. Wright heard in the news that he had been given a death sentence.

_____ Number of correct answers

Record your personal assessment of your work on the Critical Thinking Chart on page 104.

Summarizing and Paraphrasing

Follow the directions provided for question 1. Put an X in the box next to the correct answer for the other questions.

1. Reread paragraph 5 in the article. Below, write a summary of the paragraph in no more than 25 words.

_____

_____

_____

_____

Reread your summary and decide whether it covers the important ideas in the paragraph. Next, decide how to shorten the summary to 15 words or less without leaving out any essential information. Write this summary below.

_____

_____

_____

2. Read the statement from the article below. Then read the paraphrase of that statement. Choose the reason that best tells why the paraphrase does not say the same thing as the statement.

   Statement: The doctor lied to Mr. Wright about Krebiozen, but he did it because he wanted to help his patient.

   Paraphrase: Mr. Wright's doctor lied to him.

   ☐ a. Paraphrase says too much.

   ☐ b. Paraphrase doesn't say enough.

   ☐ c. Paraphrase doesn't agree with the statement.

3. Choose the sentence that correctly restates the following sentence from the article: "[Dr. West] was supposed to use [the drug] only on patients who were expected to live three months or longer."

   ☐ a. Dr. West knew that the drug was reserved for patients who would probably live at least three months.

   ☐ b. It was illegal for Dr. West to give the drug to patients who might live three months or longer.

   ☐ c. Dr. West knew that the drug would only work with patients who were supposed to live for three months or longer.

   _____ Number of correct answers

   Record your personal assessment of your work on the Critical Thinking Chart on page 104.

Critical Thinking

Put an X in the box next to the correct answer for questions 1 and 4. Follow the directions provided for the other questions.

1. From the article, you can predict that if Mr. Wright hadn't heard that doctors had given up on Krebiozen, he

   ☐ a. would have died sooner.

   ☐ b. might have lived much longer.

   ☐ c. would have stopped taking it.

2. Choose from the letters below to correctly complete the following statement. Write the letters on the lines.

In the article, _____ and _____ are alike.

a. Mr. Wright's condition before taking Krebiozen

b. Mr. Wright's condition just after taking Krebiozen for the first time

c. Mr. Wright's condition after he heard that doctors had given up on Krebiozen

3. Think about cause-effect relationships in the article. Fill in the blanks in the cause-effect chart, drawing from the letters below.

Cause	Effect
Krebiozen had been called a wonder drug. Mr. Wright heard that some doctors said Krebiozen was worthless.	_____ _____
_____	Mr. Wright recovered temporarily again.

a. Mr. Wright became ill again.

b. Mr. Wright pleaded for a chance to try Krebiozen.

c. Mr. Wright was given "fresh" Krebiozen.

4. If you were a doctor, how could you use the information in the article to treat your patients?

☐ a. Like Dr. West, lie to your patients.

☐ b. Give new drugs only to patients who you know will survive.

☐ c. Help your patients feel hopeful about recovering from their illnesses.

_____ Number of correct answers

Record your personal assessment of your work on the Critical Thinking Chart on page 104.

Personal Response

How do you think Dr. West felt when Mr. Wright improved the second time, that is, after Krebiozen had been found worthless for other patients?

_____

_____

_____

Self-Assessment

I can't really understand how _____

_____

_____

_____

Ghost Ship in the Sky

It was his best year ever. In June 1999 Payne Stewart sank a dramatic 15-foot putt on the last hole to win the U.S. Open golf championship. Stewart also won at Pebble Beach. That meant the professional golfer had won close to $12 million in his career. Over the years Stewart had had some ups and downs. At times he played well. At other times he didn't. But now everything seemed to be falling into place. "I'm so much more

In 1999 professional golfer Payne Stewart was having one of the best years of his life. He was winning steadily. But his winning streak came to an abrupt end on a strange, tragic jet flight.

at peace with myself than I've ever been in my life," Stewart said after his win in the Open.

2   By late October the golf season was almost over. There was just one big tournament left. It was the Tour Championship to be held in Houston, Texas. On October 25 Stewart and five others left Orlando, Florida. At 9:19 A.M. they took off in a private plane—a Learjet 35. They planned to fly to Dallas, Texas. There, Stewart wanted to see some land where he might build a golf course. After that he would fly on to Houston.

3   At first the flight seemed normal. After about 25 minutes, the plane reached 39,000 feet. That was its cruising altitude. At that point the aircraft leveled off. It would stay at that height until the pilot got ready to land.

4   A few more minutes passed. But then strange things began to happen. First, the pilot didn't turn left. He was supposed to steer the jet west toward Texas. Instead, the jet kept flying northwest. Second, it didn't stay level. It started climbing again. Soon it had climbed to 44,000 feet.

5   Air traffic controllers were watching their radar screens. They couldn't believe what they were seeing. Their job was to keep the skies safe. Among other things, they made sure planes didn't hit each other. They knew the altitude and direction that each plane was supposed to use. When Stewart's jet veered off course, they became alarmed. Controllers tried to radio the pilot of Stewart's plane. They tried many times, but there was no answer. It was as if no one was flying the plane.

6   What was wrong? Were the people on the plane alive or dead? Someone had to find out. So several Air Force jets were sent out after Stewart's plane. In addition, President Bill Clinton was told about the runaway jet. The President could have ordered the Air Force to shoot down the plane if it posed a clear threat to other aircraft or to people on the ground. For now, that didn't seem to be the case, but who knew what the out-of-control plane would do next?

7   One Air Force pilot maneuvered his jet within 50 feet of Stewart's plane. He looked over at the plane, which seemed to be in fine shape. He didn't see anything broken on the outside. There were no missing pieces. He took a close look at the cockpit, but couldn't see the pilot. A coating of frost on the window blocked his view. The frost meant that it was very cold inside Stewart's plane.

8   Later, another Air Force pilot got close to Stewart's jet. Colonel Rufus Forrest shadowed the jet for many miles. "It was like it was a ghost airplane," Forrest reported. "It appeared to be in perfect condition. It was flying straight and smooth, like nothing at all was wrong."

9   But something was wrong. Somehow, Stewart's jet had lost all of its cabin pressure. That seemed to be the only explanation. Any high-flying plane needs cabin pressure. At high altitudes the air temperature is far below zero. In addition, the air contains little oxygen. Cabin pressure pumps oxygen through the plane. It also keeps the cabin warm.

10   When the pressure disappears, so does the oxygen and the heat. Passengers have less than a minute before they pass out from lack of

oxygen. No one knows why this would have happened to Stewart's plane. The aircraft was in great shape. It had never had any problems. Still, for some reason the jet must have lost its cabin pressure. Within a few seconds everyone on board probably passed out. A few minutes after that, they all must have been dead.

11 Before the pilot lost consciousness, he turned on the autopilot. That device keeps a plane moving steadily even if no one is steering it. In essence, then, Stewart's jet was flying itself. It was just a question of when it would run out of fuel.

12 Forrest found it hard to watch the plane as it flew aimlessly along. "It was a helpless, eerie feeling," he said. He knew that sooner or later the jet was going to crash. Later, Forrest said that this was one mission he was "never going to forget."

13 At last Stewart's plane did run out of fuel. By then it was a long way from Texas. In fact, it was over Mina, South Dakota. It had traveled a total of about 1,400 miles.

14 When the fuel ran out, the jet was going close to 600 miles per hour. But without fuel, it just dropped out of the sky. At 1:24 P.M. the plane crashed to the ground. When it hit the ground, all Forrest saw was a "quick flash."

15 Anyone watching TV or listening to the radio knew about the tragedy as it unfolded. Stewart's wife, Tracey, knew. She tried again and again to reach her husband on his cell phone. There was no answer.

16 Ken Dunn lived in Mina, South Dakota. He also heard what was happening. He knew the runaway jet was headed his way. As Dunn stepped outside, he saw a streak of white smoke in the sky. It came from Stewart's jet. The jet had just run out of fuel and was falling fast. "It started flopping and going crazy," said Dunn. "Then it just came straight down."

17 Dunn jumped into his Jeep and drove to the crash site. After reaching the plane, he dialed 911. But he knew there was no hope. Clearly everyone on board was dead. There were just bits and pieces of the plane scattered about. The only part that was recognizable was the tail.

18 "If you didn't know it was a crash site," said one police officer, "you'd think you stumbled across a trash pile."

19 John Beck, another local resident, also rushed to the scene. "I've seen auto wrecks that were awful," he said, "but here there was no sign of any bodies."

20 The plane had blasted a huge hole in the ground. Luckily it hit in the middle of an open field. And so, as bad as the tragedy was, it could have been worse. The jet could have crashed on a highway or into homes. Still, it was a devastating loss for the victims' families. It was also a terrible loss for the world of golf. The game had lost one of its great stars.

A | Finding the Main Idea

One statement below expresses the main idea of the article. One statement is too general, or too broad. The other statement explains only part of the article; it is too narrow. Label the statements using the following key:

M—Main Idea   **B—Too Broad**   **N—Too Narrow**

_____ 1. Golfer Payne Stewart and five other passengers boarded a Learjet 35 bound from Orlando, Florida, to Dallas, Texas, at 9:19 A.M. on October 25, 1999, not knowing what lay ahead.

_____ 2. Golfer Payne Stewart died in a strange plane crash in which the plane flew by itself for hours before crashing into the ground, killing all on board.

_____ 3. In October 1999 golfer Payne Stewart died in an unusual way.

_____ Score 15 points for a correct M answer.

_____ Score 5 points for each correct B or N answer.

_____ **Total Score:** Finding the Main Idea

B | Recalling Facts

How well do you remember the facts in the article? Put an X in the box next to the answer that correctly completes each statement about the article.

1. Payne Stewart was on his way to a big golf tournament in
   ☐ a. Houston, Texas.
   ☐ b. Dallas, Texas.
   ☐ c. Palm Beach, California.

2. The first people on the ground to notice that the plane was acting strange were
   ☐ a. local residents of Mina, South Dakota.
   ☐ b. Stewart's family.
   ☐ c. air traffic controllers.

3. The frost that one pilot saw on the Learjet 35's window meant that
   ☐ a. people inside the plane were smoking.
   ☐ b. the inside of the plane was very cold.
   ☐ c. the inside of the plane was hot and humid.

4. Just before he passed out, the pilot of Stewart's plane
   ☐ a. turned on the autopilot.
   ☐ b. sent an emergency message to the Dallas control tower.
   ☐ c. tried to bring the plane lower, into warmer air.

5. The plane finally crashed
   ☐ a. into a group of homes.
   ☐ b. on a busy highway.
   ☐ c. in an open field.

Score 5 points for each correct answer.

_____ **Total Score:** Recalling Facts

C | Making Inferences

When you combine your own experience with information from a text to draw a conclusion that is not directly stated in that text, you are making an inference. Below are five statements that may or may not be inferences based on information in the article. Label the statements using the following key:

C—Correct Inference   **F—Faulty Inference**

_____ 1. The pilot of Stewart's plane didn't check the plane over carefully before leaving the ground.

_____ 2. Stewart was probably dead when the plane crashed.

_____ 3. When a plane traveling at high speed crashes, it breaks up into small pieces.

_____ 4. Air traffic controllers knew exactly where the plane would come down.

_____ 5. If the pilot had opened the windows on the jet, he could have seen well enough to land the plane safely.

Score 5 points for each correct answer.

_____ **Total Score:** Making Inferences

D | Using Words Precisely

Each numbered sentence below contains an underlined word or phrase from the article. Following the sentence are three definitions. One definition is closest to the meaning of the underlined word. One definition is opposite or nearly opposite. Label those two definitions using the following key; do not label the remaining definition.

C—Closest   **O—Opposite or Nearly Opposite**

1. In June 1999 Payne Stewart sank a <u>dramatic</u> 15-foot putt on the last hole to win the U.S. Open golf championship.

_____ a. boring

_____ b. easy

_____ c. exciting

2. When Stewart's jet <u>veered off course</u>, they became alarmed.

_____ a. turned away from the scheduled route

_____ b. stopped without warning

_____ c. continued along the expected path

3. One Air Force pilot <u>maneuvered</u> his jet within 50 feet of Stewart's plane.

_____ a. left

_____ b. drove poorly and clumsily

_____ c. moved skillfully

4. Forrest found it hard to watch the plane as it flew <u>aimlessly</u> along.

_____ a. with a clear purpose in mind

_____ b. without a goal

_____ c. slowly

5. "It was a helpless, <u>eerie</u> feeling," he said.

_____ a. spooky

_____ b. normal and natural

_____ c. silly

_____ Score 3 points for each correct C answer.

_____ Score 2 points for each correct O answer.

_____ **Total Score:** Using Words Precisely

Enter the four total scores in the spaces below, and add them together to find your Reading Comprehension Score. Then record your score on the graph on page 103.

Score	Question Type	Lesson 8
_____	Finding the Main Idea	
_____	Recalling Facts	
_____	Making Inferences	
_____	Using Words Precisely	
_____	**Reading Comprehension Score**	

Author's Approach

Put an X in the box next to the correct answer.

1. What is the authors' purpose in writing "Ghost Ship in the Sky"?

☐ a. to express an opinion about the safety of air travel

☐ b. to inform the reader about Payne Stewart's lifetime income

☐ c. to describe a situation in which a well-known person died in a strange accident

2. Which of the following statements from the article best describes the crash site?

☐ a. The plane had blasted a huge hole in the ground.

☐ b. And so, as bad as the tragedy was, it could have been worse.

☐ c. The jet could have crashed on a highway or into homes.

3. In this article, "After reaching the plane, he [Dunn] dialed 911" means

☐ a. Dunn phoned the newspapers when he saw that it was Payne Stewart's plane that had crashed.

☐ b. Dunn tried to contact the pilot of the plane.

☐ c. Dunn called for help after he saw the crash.

4. The authors tell this story mainly by

☐ a. comparing different topics.

☐ b. telling about events in the order they happened.

☐ c. telling different stories about the same topic.

_____ Number of correct answers

Record your personal assessment of your work on the Critical Thinking Chart on page 104.

Summarizing and Paraphrasing

Put an X in the box next to the correct answer for questions 1 and 3. Follow the directions provided for question 2.

1. Below are summaries of the article. Choose the summary that says all the most important things about the article, but in the fewest words.

    ☐ a. Payne Stewart was a well-known golfer who was finally playing well and winning tournaments. He boarded a plane in Florida bound for Texas. After the plane started acting strangely, air traffic controllers became worried. The plane crashed about 1,400 miles off course.

    ☐ b. In 1999 Golfer Payne Stewart died in a strange plane crash. For some unknown reason, everyone on board became unconscious, and the plane continued to fly unattended for hours. Finally, the plane crashed in a field.

    ☐ c. No one can figure out why Payne Stewart's jet crashed in a South Dakota field when it was on the way to Dallas, Texas, from Orlando, Florida, in 1999.

2. Reread paragraph 4 in the article. Below, write a summary of the paragraph in no more than 25 words.

    _____

    _____

    _____

    _____

Reread your summary and decide whether it covers the important ideas in the paragraph. Next, decide how to shorten the summary to 15 words or less without leaving out any essential information. Write this summary below.

_____

_____

_____

3. Read the statement about the article below. Then read the paraphrase of that statement. Choose the reason that best tells why the paraphrase does not say the same thing as the statement.

    Statement: One Air Force pilot got close enough to the plane to report that there was nothing broken on the outside.

    Paraphrase: One Air Force pilot said there was nothing wrong with the plane.

    ☐ a. Paraphrase says too much.

    ☐ b. Paraphrase doesn't say enough.

    ☐ c. Paraphrase doesn't agree with the statement.

    _____ Number of correct answers

    Record your personal assessment of your work on the Critical Thinking Chart on page 104.

Critical Thi[nking]

[handwritten note: ⑦ packets stapled p. 79-83]

Follow the direc[tions] [for questions 1, 2, 3,] and 4. Put an X in the box next to [the answer to the oth]er questions.

1. Choose fro[m the words below to] complete the following st[atement. Write them on th]e lines.

   On the positive side, _____, but on the negative side _____.

   a. several people died in the crash

   b. the plane didn't crash into a crowded neighborhood or onto a freeway

   c. the plane was bound for Dallas, Texas

2. What was the cause of the jet's plunge to the ground?

   ☐ a. The jet exploded in midair.

   ☐ b. The autopilot stopped working.

   ☐ c. The jet ran out of fuel.

3. How is "Ghost Ship in the Sky" an example of a bizarre ending?

   ☐ a. Before the crash that killed everyone on board, the plane flew perfectly, as if a ghost were at the controls.

   ☐ b. Payne Stewart, a famous golfer, was among the passengers who died when the plane crashed.

   ☐ c. The plane must have had a serious problem that made it lose its cabin pressure.

4. In which paragraph did you find your information or details to

   answer question 2? _____

   | _____ Number of correct answers |

   Record your personal assessment of your work on the Critical Thinking Chart on page 104.

Personal Response

What was most surprising or interesting to you about this article?

_____

_____

_____

_____

Self-Assessment

One of the things I did best when reading this article was _____

_____

I believe I did this well because _____

_____

_____

Lost in the Arctic

Sir John Franklin knew how to survive in the Arctic. Over the years, he had made three trips there in search of the North Pole. Now, in 1845, he wanted to make one more journey north. He wanted to find the Northwest Passage.

2   No one knew for sure that the Northwest Passage existed. But everyone assumed it did. It was supposed to be a water route over the top of North America. Ships could use it to sail from the Atlantic Ocean to

In 1857 Captain Francis McClintock and his crew set out for the Arctic to find out the fate of the Franklin expedition. This sketch depicting McClintock's meeting with the Inuits at Cape Victoria was made by one of the officers of the expedition.

the Pacific. Then they wouldn't have to go all the way down around South America. Many countries were eager to find the passage. Franklin wanted to help his country, Great Britain, get to it first.

3   The British navy knew that Franklin was an old pro at Arctic expeditions. In fact, some navy officials thought he was *too* old. He was, after all, 59. But Franklin had his heart set on getting the job. William Parry, a colleague, wrote the navy to support him. "[Franklin] is a fitter man to go than any I know," Parry wrote. "If you don't let him go, the old man will die of disappointment."

4   In the end, Franklin got the job. The navy did all it could to help him prepare for the expedition. It gave him two of its best ships—the *Erebus* and the *Terror*. These ships had been tested in Arctic waters. Their reinforced hulls would protect them from polar ice. Franklin also got a handpicked crew of 128 men. In addition, the navy supplied him with enough food and fuel to last three years.

5   Franklin and his men set sail on May 19, 1845. People knew they would be gone for a long time. So when no news came in 1846, it wasn't a surprise. Franklin had no reliable way to communicate. He did have 200 message bottles. He could drop them in the sea and hope that someone found them. But none of the bottles turned up.

6   Another summer and winter passed. Still there was no news from Franklin. Now a few people began to worry. They wondered if something had gone wrong. They even urged the navy to send a rescue mission. But navy officials decided to wait. After all, other Arctic explorers had gone longer without a word, and they had all come back. The navy saw no reason to panic.

7   A third winter came and went. Again, there was no news. Now even navy officials grew concerned. In 1848 the navy sent two ships to find Franklin. The rescue squads searched the Arctic for more than a year. But they found no sign of Franklin or his men. And so it became clear to everyone: something *had* gone wrong in the Arctic.

8   In 1850 the government offered a large reward to anyone who could find the Franklin expedition. Franklin's wife, Lady Jane Franklin, offered her own reward. Soon 15 search parties went looking. It was like a mad race. Everyone wanted to collect the rewards. Before it was all over, 40 search parties joined in the hunt. One group found a campsite but little else.

9   Then, in 1853, a searcher named John Rae met some Inuit natives. They told him about a band of white men they had seen. The white men's ships had become stuck in the ice. The Inuits had seen the men dragging a small boat across the snow.

10   The Inuits led Rae to a camp used by the white men. There Rae made a gruesome discovery. He found 30 bodies. Some were in tents, some were in the snow, and some were under the small boat. Many of the bodies had been badly mutilated. Had the men tried to survive by eating the flesh of the dead? Just the thought made navy officials sick.

11   Rae got his reward, and navy officials declared the case closed. From their point of view, they now knew more than enough. But Lady Jane Franklin refused to accept the bad

news. She clung to the hope that some of the men might still be alive. Even if they weren't, she wanted their bodies brought back. "The bones of the dead," she pleaded, "should be sought. Their last written words [should be] saved from destruction."

12   The navy ignored her requests, but Lady Jane Franklin didn't give up. Instead, she asked friends for help. Quickly funds came pouring in. Using this money plus her own, she sent one more rescue squad north. She put Francis McClintock in command. He was a tough veteran of the Arctic. If anyone could find Franklin, he could.

13   On July 1, 1857, McClintock set sail. He and his crew of 25 spent more than two years searching for Franklin. In the fall of 1859, McClintock's boat, the *Fox*, got trapped in the ice. McClintock could hear its timbers groan as the ice pressed against it. He was terrified that the ship would be crushed. "I can understand how a man's hair can turn grey in a few hours," he wrote in his diary.

14   The *Fox* remained trapped in the ice for 242 days. During that time, McClintock and his men explored a nearby island on foot. One of the men discovered a cairn. (A cairn is a pile of rocks. Explorers used cairns to bury

their records for others to find.) Inside the cairn was a tin box containing two messages. One was dated May 28, 1847. It was signed by a member of Franklin's crew. The message gave the crew's position and ended with the words "All well."

15   This was a cheerful note. But the second message dashed any hopes that Franklin was still alive. It was written in the margins of the first note. The date on this second message was April 25, 1848. It read, in part, "*Terror* and *Erebus* were deserted on 22 April." The message went on to add, "Sir John Franklin died on 11 June 1847. Total loss by deaths in the expedition to this date, nine officers and 15 men."

16   Soon after that, McClintock and his men found other bodies from the Franklin expedition. They also talked to local Inuits. Slowly, the fate of Franklin's men grew clear. When the *Erebus* and *Terror* became stuck in the ice, the crews had abandoned the ships. They had begun to walk south, dragging a small boat filled with supplies. At night they pitched tents and huddled together to stay warm. But they faced hundreds of miles of frozen wilderness. The men fell one by one and died as they went. In the end, they were all dead.

17   The Franklin expedition had begun with the highest hopes, but it had ended in tragedy. The McClintock search party was the last one sent out. Even Lady Jane Franklin accepted the sad truth. The only bright note was that the search parties added to people's knowledge of the Arctic. In fact, some rescuers actually did find the Northwest Passage. But it turned out to be too cold and ice-clogged to be used. Later, a better route to Asia was created by digging the Panama Canal, which was opened in 1914.

If you have been timed while reading this article, enter your reading time below. Then turn to the Words-per-Minute Table on page 101 and look up your reading speed (words per minute). Enter your reading speed on the graph on page 102.

Reading Time: Lesson 9

_____ : _____

Minutes   Seconds

A Finding the Main Idea

One statement below expresses the main idea of the article. One statement is too general, or too broad. The other statement explains only part of the article; it is too narrow. Label the statements using the following key:

M—Main Idea   **B—Too Broad**   **N—Too Narrow**

_____ 1. Exploring the Arctic during the 19th century was a daring and dangerous adventure.

_____ 2. British navy officials let Sir John Franklin use two of their ships to search for the Northwest Passage.

_____ 3. Sir John Franklin's Arctic expedition to find the Northwest Passage ended in tragedy.

_____ Score 15 points for a correct M answer.

_____ Score 5 points for each correct B or N answer.

_____ **Total Score:** Finding the Main Idea

B Recalling Facts

How well do you remember the facts in the article? Put an X in the box next to the answer that correctly completes each statement about the article.

1. The navy supplied Franklin with food for
   - ☐ a. 3 years.
   - ☐ b. 6 months.
   - ☐ c. 10 years.

2. Most people searched for the Franklin expedition because they
   - ☐ a. loved Sir John Franklin.
   - ☐ b. wanted the large reward.
   - ☐ c. needed an exciting adventure.

3. The Inuits reported seeing white men
   - ☐ a. dragging a small boat across the snow.
   - ☐ b. building a new ship.
   - ☐ c. making a cairn for their diaries.

4. The last search party was led by
   - ☐ a. John Rae.
   - ☐ b. Sir John Franklin.
   - ☐ c. Francis McClintock.

5. Ships can now sail from the Atlantic to the Pacific using the
   - ☐ a. Northwest Passage.
   - ☐ b. Panama Canal.
   - ☐ c. Erie Canal.

Score 5 points for each correct answer.

_____ **Total Score:** Recalling Facts

C | Making Inferences

When you combine your own experience and information from a text to draw a conclusion that is not directly stated in that text, you are making an inference. Below are five statements that may or may not be inferences based on information in the article. Label the statements using the following key:

C—Correct Inference   **F—Faulty Inference**

_____ 1. Since no message bottles were found, friends knew that Franklin did not drop any in the ocean.

_____ 2. Slow communication methods of the past forced people then to be more patient than people are today.

_____ 3. People in Great Britain believed that the first country to find the Northwest Passage would have an advantage over other nations.

_____ 4. Lady Jane Franklin was easily discouraged by bad news.

_____ 5. If the navy had sent a rescue mission after the second winter, Franklin and his men would have survived.

Score 5 points for each correct answer.

_____ **Total Score:** Making Inferences

D | Using Words Precisely

Each numbered sentence below contains an underlined word or phrase from the article. Following the sentence are three definitions. One definition is closest to the meaning of the underlined word. One definition is opposite or nearly opposite. Label those two definitions using the following key; do not label the remaining definition.

C—Closest   **O—Opposite or Nearly Opposite**

1. No one knew for sure that the Northwest Passage existed. But everyone <u>assumed</u> it did.

_____ a. believed

_____ b. hoped

_____ c. doubted

2. William Parry, a <u>colleague</u>, wrote the navy to support him.

_____ a. teacher

_____ b. stranger

_____ c. co-worker

3. Franklin had no <u>reliable</u> way to communicate.

_____ a. uncertain

_____ b. pleasant

_____ c. dependable

4. Many of the bodies had been badly <u>mutilated</u>.

_____ a. shaken

_____ b. cut up; damaged

_____ c. made whole and perfect

5. "The bones of the dead," she pleaded, "should be <u>sought</u>."

_____ a. avoided

_____ b. buried

_____ c. searched for

_____ Score 3 points for each correct C answer.

_____ Score 2 points for each correct O answer.

_____ **Total Score:** Using Words Precisely

Enter the four total scores in the spaces below, and add them together to find your Reading Comprehension Score. Then record your score on the graph on page 103.

Score	Question Type	Lesson 9
_____	Finding the Main Idea	
_____	Recalling Facts	
_____	Making Inferences	
_____	Using Words Precisely	
_____	**Reading Comprehension Score**	

Author's Approach

Put an X in the box next to the correct answer.

1. The authors use the first sentence of the article to

☐ a. introduce the reader to Sir John Franklin.

☐ b. compare the climates of the Arctic and England.

☐ c. entertain the reader with a simple story.

2. Which of the following statements from the article best describes Francis McClintock's qualifications as an explorer?

☐ a. During that time, McClintock and his men explored a nearby island on foot.

☐ b. [McClintock] was terrified that the ship would be crushed.

☐ c. [McClintock] was a tough veteran of the Arctic. If anyone could find Franklin, he could.

3. Choose the statement below that best describes the authors' position in paragraph 17.

☐ a. Lady Jane Franklin was a stubborn woman.

☐ b. The Franklin expedition was tragic, but it increased people's knowledge of the Arctic.

☐ c. The McClintock search party was the only one that tried hard to find the Franklin expedition.

_____ Number of correct answers

Record your personal assessment of your work on the Critical Thinking Chart on page 104.

Summarizing and Paraphrasing

Follow the directions provided for questions 1 and 2.

1. Look for the important ideas and events in paragraphs 3 and 4. Summarize those paragraphs in one or two sentences.

_____

_____

_____

2. Complete the following one-sentence summary of the article using the lettered phrases from the phrase bank below. Write the letters on the lines.

> ### Phrase Bank
> a. the discovery of the fate of the Franklin expedition
> b. a description of the planning and beginning of the Franklin expedition
> c. efforts taken to find the lost explorers

The article "Lost in the Arctic" begins with _____, goes on

to explain _____, and ends with _____.

> _____ Number of correct answers
>
> Record your personal assessment of your work on the Critical Thinking Chart on page 104.

Critical Thinking

Follow the directions provided for questions 1, 2, and 5. Put an X in the box next to the correct answer for the other questions.

1. For each statement below, write *O* if it expresses an opinion or write *F* if it expresses a fact.

_____ a. Lady Jane Franklin should not have wasted her money and risked other people's lives to find her husband's lost expedition.

_____ b. Sir John Franklin was not a very skillful commander.

_____ c. John McClintock's ship was trapped in the ice for 242 days.

2. Choose from the letters below to correctly complete the following statement. Write the letters on the lines.

On the positive side, _____, but on the negative side

_____.

a. Franklin's expedition ended in tragedy

b. Franklin's expedition helped people learn more about the Arctic

c. navy officials expected the Franklin expedition to be back in about three years

3. What was the cause of Franklin's crew abandoning their ships?

☐ a. The ships exploded.

☐ b. The ships were stuck in the ice.

☐ c. The ships sank.

4. How is "Lost in the Arctic" related to the theme of *Bizarre Endings*?

☐ a. The loss of such a well-planned expedition led by an old pro was very unusual.

☐ b. The expedition was led by an experienced Arctic explorer.

☐ c. The British government and Franklin's wife offered rewards to anyone who could find the expedition.

5. In which paragraph did you find your information or details to answer question 3? _____

_____ Number of correct answers

Record your personal assessment of your work on the Critical Thinking Chart on page 104.

Personal Response

I know the feeling that Lady Jane Franklin had when she refused to give up her search because _____

_____

_____

_____

Self-Assessment

One good question about this article that was not asked would be,

_____

_____

The answer is _____

_____

_____

The Curse of the Hope Diamond

Jean Baptiste Tavernier's eyes lit up when he saw it. An expert on rare gems, he stared at the diamond. It was huge. It was bigger than any diamond he had ever seen before. Its color was "a beautiful violet."

There was just one problem. The diamond was embedded in a statue of the Hindu god Rama Sita. The glittering jewel decorated the god's forehead.

2 Tavernier approached the priests who watched over the statue. He asked if they would sell him the diamond. They said no. But Tavernier couldn't bear the thought of leaving India

As diamonds go, the Hope diamond is not particularly large or costly. However, it has managed to gain quite a bad reputation among its previous owners.

without it. So he ordered his men to tie up the priests. Then Tavernier pried the gem out of the statue and ran away.

3 No one is sure if this story is true. It is said to have taken place in 1642. But the life of Tavernier is shrouded in mystery. What we do know is that one way or another, Tavernier got his hands on the diamond.

4 We also know something else. For some strange reason, bad luck seemed to follow the diamond wherever it went. Was it sheer coincidence? Or was there more to it? Some people said that Rama Sita wanted revenge for the theft of the diamond. They said this god put a curse on the jewel.

5 Tavernier himself certainly came to an ugly end. In 1668 he sold the gem to King Louis XIV of France. After that he lost all his money. He moved to Russia. There he was attacked and killed by a pack of wild dogs. Louis XIV didn't do so well, either. He died a slow and painful death from smallpox. Was the "curse" of the stolen diamond to blame?

6 Back when Tavernier had the diamond, it was roughly cut and

weighed 112½ carats. (Diamonds and other gems are measured in carats. A 112-carat gem is enormous. It would be about the size of a hen's egg.) Louis XIV had his jeweler cut the diamond into three pieces. This gave each piece a greater shine. Reflecting light now made the pieces appear blue. The largest piece was cut in the shape of a heart. It weighed 67 carats and was called the French Blue. It was the most dazzling of the royal jewels.

7 In 1774 Louis XVI inherited this blue diamond. His wife, Marie Antoinette, wore it often. But in 1789 the "curse" struck again. The French people rose up in revolt. They turned against Louis and Marie. In 1793 they killed these two rulers by cutting off their heads.

8 The rebels put the blue diamond in a glass case for safekeeping. But it wasn't guarded very well. In 1792 someone walked off with it. The French Blue was never seen again.

9 Most experts believe it was taken to Spain and cut once again. Perhaps whoever had the French Blue knew that it was too famous to sell as it was. In any case, a piece of it resurfaced as

an oval blue diamond. This one weighed 45½ carats. In 1830 it came into the hands of a rich banker named Henry Philip Hope. From this point on, the stone was called the Hope Diamond.

10   Although the diamond had a new name, the old "curse" still seemed to be at work. Henry died without marrying. The diamond passed to his nephew's grandson, Sir Francis Hope. Francis married an American actress named May Yohe. So far, so good. But after a few years, May ran off with another man. Francis's life went from bad to worse. He went bankrupt and had to sell the diamond. Even so, he died in poverty. And the "curse" didn't spare May Yohe. She spent her last days scrubbing floors to make a living.

11   The next owner of the Hope diamond was a New York jeweler named Joseph Frankels. He, too, went broke. The diamond then passed from one person to the next. Simon Montharides, a Greek gem merchant, had it for a time. But he, his wife, and their children all died in a mountain accident. They fell off a cliff. For a while, the Sultan of Turkey, Abdul Hamid, owned the stone. But like Louis XVI, he was overthrown in a revolution.

12   A Russian prince named Kanitovski bought the diamond. He gave it to a French singer named Lorens Laduc. It was said that Kanitovski loved Laduc. But the day after giving her the diamond, he killed her. He himself was later stabbed to death.

13   Despite the "curse" of the Hope diamond, people still wanted to own it. In 1912 an American named Evalyn McLean bought the Hope diamond. She paid $154,000 for it.

14   McLean didn't believe in the "curse." To her, all the death and dying that surrounded the gem was just bad luck. McLean wore the Hope diamond almost all the time. When she didn't have it on, she stuffed it in a cushion. She hired a guard to keep it from being stolen.

15   Perhaps Evalyn McLean should have hired a second guard to watch over herself and her family. After all, some would say the "curse" had not yet run its course. McLean's son died in a car crash. Her daughter died from an overdose of sleeping pills. She and her husband nearly divorced. He spent his last days in a hospital for the mentally ill.

16   Evalyn McLean herself died in 1947. With her death, the "curse" of the Hope diamond seems to have ended. Harry Winston bought the stone two years later. For about 10 years, he showed the Hope diamond in exhibits around the world. Then, in 1958, he gave it to the Smithsonian Institution. Believe it or not, Winston sent this priceless gem through the mail. He spent just $2.44 on postage! Luckily, it arrived safely.

17   The Hope diamond has been on public display ever since it got to the Smithsonian. It is one of the top tourist sights in Washington, D.C. Each day, thousands of people line up to see it. No tragic pattern has been found among those who view the diamond. Does that mean Rama Sita's "curse" has finally been lifted? Or does evil still lurk within that beautiful blue stone?

If you have been timed while reading this article, enter your reading time below. Then turn to the Words-per-Minute Table on page 101 and look up your reading speed (words per minute). Enter your reading speed on the graph on page 102.

Reading Time: Lesson 10

_____ : _____
Minutes   Seconds

A | Finding the Main Idea

One statement below expresses the main idea of the article. One statement is too general, or too broad. The other statement explains only part of the article; it is too narrow. Label the statements using the following key:

M—Main Idea   **B—Too Broad**   **N—Too Narrow**

_____ 1. So many awful things have happened to owners of the Hope diamond over the last three centuries that many people believe there is a curse on the jewel.

_____ 2. Many mysterious and tragic stories are connected to the beautiful blue jewel known as the Hope diamond.

_____ 3. The Hope diamond got its name from one of its owners, Henry Philip Hope, who left the jewel to his nephew's grandson.

_____ Score 15 points for a correct M answer.

_____ Score 5 points for each correct B or N answer.

_____ **Total Score:** Finding the Main Idea

B | Recalling Facts

How well do you remember the facts in the article? Put an X in the box next to the answer that correctly completes each statement about the article.

1. Jean Baptiste Tavernier was said to have
   □ a. embedded a huge jewel in a statue.
   □ b. cut a huge jewel into three parts.
   □ c. stolen a huge jewel from India.

2. The huge diamond was cut into pieces to
   □ a. disguise the stolen jewel.
   □ b. give each piece a greater shine.
   □ c. remove the "curse" from it.

3. The jewel called the French Blue
   □ a. disappeared after the French Revolution.
   □ b. was the size of a hen's egg.
   □ c. was sold by Louis XIV.

4. The Hope diamond
   □ a. is the French Blue under a new name.
   □ b. is a large piece of the French Blue.
   □ c. was too famous to sell.

5. Harry Winston bought the Hope diamond
   □ a. for $154,000.
   □ b. in 1947.
   □ c. and donated it to the Smithsonian Institution.

Score 5 points for each correct answer.

_____ **Total Score:** Recalling Facts

C Making Inferences

When you combine your own experience and information from a text to draw a conclusion that is not directly stated in that text, you are making an inference. Below are five statements that may or may not be inferences based on information in the article. Label the statements using the following key:

C—Correct Inference   **F—Faulty Inference**

_____ 1. The statue from which Tavernier reportedly stole the diamond was quite large, probably larger than an average human being.

_____ 2. At the time of Louis XIV, there was no known cure for smallpox.

_____ 3. If Louis XVI and Marie Antoinette had not owned the French Blue, they would not have been overthrown.

_____ 4. A large jewel loses most, if not all, of its value if it is cut into pieces.

_____ 5. Harry Winston, the last private owner of the Hope diamond, put great trust in the U.S. mail.

Score 5 points for each correct answer.

_____ **Total Score:** Making Inferences

D Using Words Precisely

Each numbered sentence below contains an underlined word or phrase from the article. Following the sentence are three definitions. One definition is closest to the meaning of the underlined word. One definition is opposite or nearly opposite. Label those two definitions using the following key; do not label the remaining definition.

C—Closest   **O—Opposite or Nearly Opposite**

1. The diamond was <u>embedded in</u> a statue of the Hindu god Rama Sita.

_____ a. set loose; separated from

_____ b. set in

_____ c. compared with

2. Then Tavernier <u>pried</u> the gem out of the statue and ran away.

_____ a. washed

_____ b. made firm and unable to be moved

_____ c. obtained with difficulty, as by forcing with a tool

3. But the life of Tavernier is <u>shrouded</u> in mystery.

_____ a. made clear

_____ b. reported

_____ c. hidden

4. For a while, the Sultan of Turkey, Abdul Hamid, owned the stone. But like Louis XVI, he was <u>overthrown</u> in a revolution.

_____ a. wrapped up

_____ b. restored

_____ c. removed from power

5. No <u>tragic</u> pattern has been found among those who view the diamond.

_____ a. dreadful

_____ b. orderly

_____ c. amusing; cheery

_____ Score 3 points for each correct C answer.

_____ Score 2 points for each correct O answer.

_____ **Total Score:** Using Words Precisely

Enter the four total scores in the spaces below, and add them together to find your Reading Comprehension Score. Then record your score on the graph on page 103.

Score	Question Type	Lesson 10
_____	Finding the Main Idea	
_____	Recalling Facts	
_____	Making Inferences	
_____	Using Words Precisely	
_____	**Reading Comprehension Score**	

Author's Approach

Put an X in the box next to the correct answer.

1. What do the authors mean by the statement "Jean Baptiste Tavernier's eyes lit up when he saw it [the diamond]"?

☐ a. Light from the diamond shone into Tavernier's eyes.

☐ b. The sight of the diamond excited and delighted Tavernier.

☐ c. Tavernier started to cry when he saw the diamond.

2. Choose the statement below that is the weakest argument for wanting to own the Hope diamond.

☐ a. The Hope diamond is beautiful.

☐ b. The Hope diamond is valuable.

☐ c. Bad luck seems to follow the Hope diamond.

3. Choose the statement below that best describes the authors' position in paragraph 15.

☐ a. Evalyn McLean was an amazingly wealthy woman.

☐ b. Everyone in Evalyn McLean's family was mentally ill.

☐ c. Evalyn McLean's life was filled with tragedy.

4. The authors probably wrote this article to

☐ a. tell the legend of the Hope diamond.

☐ b. inform the reader about how valuable diamonds are cut and weighed.

☐ c. persuade the reader to visit the Smithsonian Institution to see the Hope diamond.

_____ Number of correct answers

Record your personal assessment of your work on the Critical Thinking Chart on page 104.

Summarizing and Paraphrasing

Follow the directions provided for these questions.

1. Complete the following one-sentence summary of the article using the lettered phrases from the phrase bank below. Write the letters on the lines.

> **Phrase Bank**
>
> a. how the diamond has been connected with death and bad luck
>
> b. information about where the diamond is today
>
> c. the story of how the diamond was stolen from a Hindu statue

The article "The Curse of the Hope Diamond" begins with

_____, goes on to explain _____, and ends with

_____.

2. Reread paragraph 7 in the article. Below, write a summary of the paragraph in no more than 25 words.

_____

_____

_____

_____

Reread your summary and decide whether it covers the important ideas in the paragraph. Next, decide how to shorten the summary to 15 words or less without leaving out any essential information. Write this summary below.

_____

_____

_____

_____ Number of correct answers

Record your personal assessment of your work on the Critical Thinking Chart on page 104.

Critical Thinking

Put an X in the box next to the correct answer for questions 1, 2, 4, and 5. Follow the directions provided for question 3.

1. Which of the following statements from the article is an opinion rather than a fact?

☐ a. Perhaps Evalyn McLean should have hired a second guard to watch over herself and her family.

☐ b. Diamonds and other gems are measured in carats.

☐ c. The rebels put the blue diamond in a glass case for safekeeping.

2. Considering Tavernier's actions as described in this article, you can predict that he

☐ a. often returned to the place where he stole the diamond.

☐ b. was later ashamed of himself for stealing the diamond.

☐ c. would have done almost anything to get the diamond.

3. Choose from the letters below to correctly complete the following statement. Write the letters on the lines.

According to the article, Tavernier's theft of the diamond caused _____ to _____, and the effect was _____.

a. put a curse on the diamond

b. bad luck for anyone owning the diamond

c. the god Rama Sita

4. How is "The Curse of the Hope Diamond" related to the theme of *Bizarre Endings*?

☐ a. Many people who have owned the diamond have had horrible and unexpected deaths.

☐ b. The Hope diamond was destroyed in a bizarre way.

☐ c. According to legend, the Hope diamond was stolen from the statue of the Hindu god Rama Sita.

5. What did you have to do to answer question 2?

☐ a. find a description (how something looks)

☐ b. make a prediction (what might happen next)

☐ c. find a cause (why something happened)

_____ Number of correct answers

Record your personal assessment of your work on the Critical Thinking Chart on page 104.

Personal Response

How do you think you would feel if you were suddenly the owner of the Hope diamond?

_____

_____

_____

Self-Assessment

I was confused on question _____ in section _____ because

_____

_____

_____

Compare and Contrast

Think about the articles you have read in Unit Two. Pick the three articles that make you most curious. Write the titles of the articles in the first column of the chart below. Use information you learned from the articles to fill in the empy boxes in the chart.

Title	Which details in the article were hardest to understand?	What were the strangest events that took place?	Why do you think this article was included in this book?

I would like to learn more about _____ . I want to know the answers to these questions: _____

_____

_____

Words-per-Minute Table

Unit Two

Directions: If you were timed while reading an article, refer to the Reading Time you recorded in the box at the end of the article. Use this words-per-minute table to determine your reading speed for that article. Then plot your reading speed on the graph on page 102.

Lesson No. of Words	6 1,127	7 1,032	8 1,147	9 1,189	10 1,030	
1:30	751	688	765	793	687	**90**
1:40	676	619	688	713	618	**100**
1:50	615	563	626	649	562	**110**
2:00	564	516	574	595	515	**120**
2:10	520	476	529	549	475	**130**
2:20	483	442	492	510	441	**140**
2:30	451	413	459	476	412	**150**
2:40	423	387	430	446	386	**160**
2:50	398	364	405	420	364	**170**
3:00	376	344	382	396	343	**180**
3:10	356	326	362	375	325	**190**
3:20	338	310	344	357	309	**200**
3:30	322	295	328	340	294	**210**
3:40	307	281	313	324	281	**220**
3:50	294	269	299	310	269	**230**
4:00	282	258	287	297	258	**240**
4:10	270	248	275	285	247	**250**
4:20	260	238	265	274	238	**260**
4:30	250	229	255	264	229	**270**
4:40	242	221	246	255	221	**280**
4:50	233	214	237	246	213	**290**
5:00	225	206	229	238	206	**300**
5:10	218	200	222	230	199	**310**
5:20	211	194	215	223	193	**320**
5:30	205	188	209	793	187	**330**
5:40	199	182	202	210	182	**340**
5:50	193	177	197	204	177	**350**
6:00	188	172	191	198	172	**360**
6:10	183	167	186	193	167	**370**
6:20	178	163	181	713	163	**380**
6:30	173	159	176	183	158	**390**
6:40	169	155	172	178	155	**400**
6:50	165	151	168	174	151	**410**
7:00	161	147	164	170	147	**420**
7:10	157	144	160	166	144	**430**
7:20	154	141	156	162	140	**440**
7:30	150	138	153	159	137	**450**
7:40	147	135	150	155	134	**460**
7:50	144	132	146	152	131	**470**
8:00	141	129	143	149	129	**480**

Minutes and Seconds

Seconds

Plotting Your Progress: Reading Speed

Unit Two

Directions: If you were timed while reading an article, write your words-per-minute rate for that article in the box under the number of the lesson. Then plot your reading speed on the graph by putting a small X on the line directly above the number of the lesson, across from the number of words per minute you read. As you mark your speed for each lesson, graph your progress by drawing a line to connect the X's.

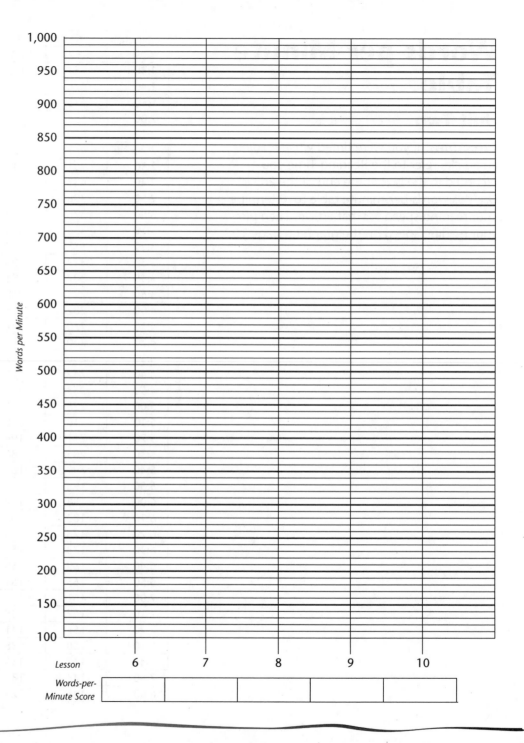

Words per Minute

Lesson	6	7	8	9	10
Words-per-Minute Score					

Plotting Your Progress: Reading Comprehension

Unit Two

Directions: Write your Reading Comprehension score for each lesson in the box under the number of the lesson. Then plot your score on the graph by putting a small X on the line directly above the number of the lesson and across from the score you earned. As you mark your score for each lesson, graph your progress by drawing a line to connect the X's.

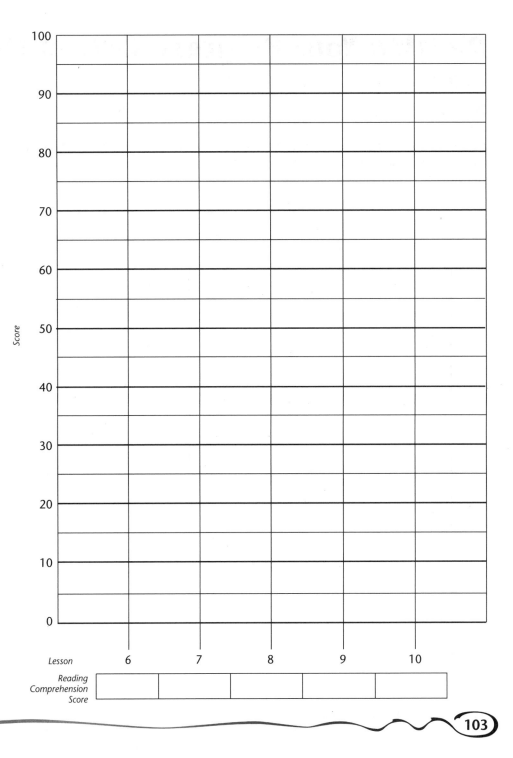

Plotting Your Progress: Critical Thinking

Unit Two

Directions: Work with your teacher to evaluate your responses to the Critical Thinking questions for each lesson. Then fill in the appropriate spaces in the chart below. For each lesson and each type of Critical Thinking question, do the following: Mark a minus sign (–) in the box to indicate areas in which you feel you could improve. Mark a plus sign (+) to indicate areas in which you feel you did well. Mark a minus-slash-plus sign (–/+) to indicate areas in which you had mixed success. Then write any comments you have about your performance, including ideas for improvement.

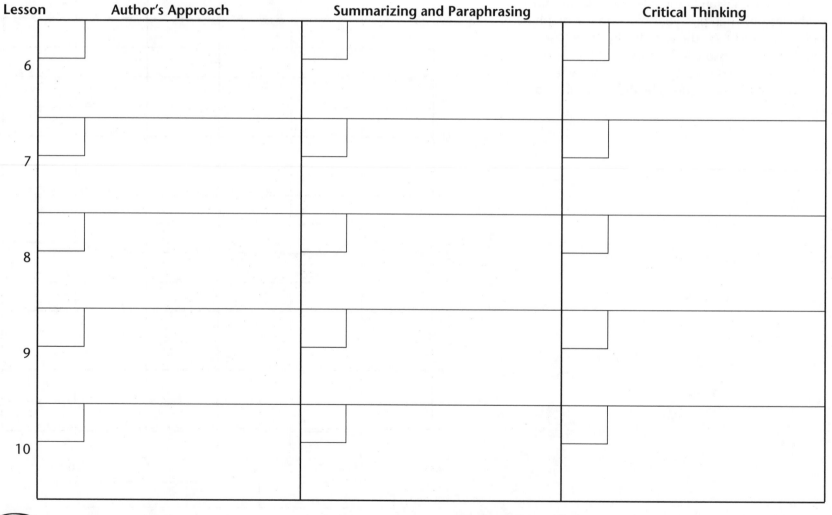

Lesson	Author's Approach	Summarizing and Paraphrasing	Critical Thinking
6			
7			
8			
9			
10			

UNIT THREE

The Last Flight of the Star Tiger

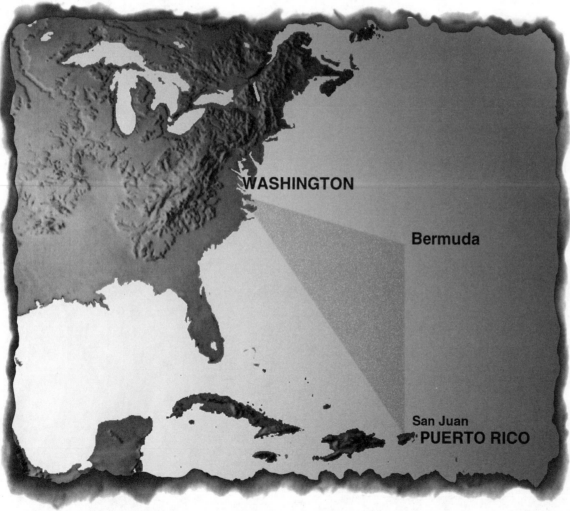

WASHINGTON

Bermuda

San Juan
PUERTO RICO

Captain Brian McMillan shook his head in dismay. He had just learned that the head winds were blowing at nearly 70 miles per hour. He knew he couldn't fly the *Star Tiger* into the teeth of those winds. So McMillan decided to wait a day. He hoped the winds would die down overnight.

[2]   The *Star Tiger* was a British plane. It had left London on January 27, 1948. The four-engine plane carried a crew of six as well as 25 passengers.

The Bermuda Triangle is an area of the Atlantic Ocean known for its strong currents and unusual magnetic forces. A remarkable number of ships and planes, such as the Star Tiger, *have been lost there, never to be seen again.*

First McMillan had flown the *Star Tiger* to Lisbon, Portugal. After an overnight stay, he took it on to Santa Maria in the Azores. (The Azores are a group of islands in the Atlantic Ocean.) Now McMillan faced a 2,000-mile flight to Bermuda. That was a long trip in those days. In fact, it was the longest airline flight over open ocean at the time.

3   McMillan was in the Azores when he got the bad news about the winds. Generally, he didn't worry about flying to Bermuda. The weather there was always warm, so there was no fear that the wings would ice up. But these head winds worried McMillan. Strong winds could blow a plane far off course. Also, bucking such tough winds slows a plane down and eats up its fuel. A similar plane had recently arrived in Bermuda with its gas gauge on empty. The pilot almost had to ditch the plane in the sea. So Captain McMillan, a seasoned pilot, knew the risks. And he wasn't about to take any unnecessary chances.

4   The next day, things looked better. The winds had died down. To make sure he had plenty of fuel, McMillan ordered his tanks filled "to the gills."

That gave him enough fuel to fly an extra $3^1/_2$ hours.

5   The *Star Tiger* took off at 3:34 P.M. on January 29. The flight was expected to take $12^1/_2$ hours. Most of the flying would be done at night. That way, McMillan's navigator could use the stars to find the plane's position.

6   A cargo plane left an hour before the *Star Tiger*. The cargo plane was flown by Captain Frank Griffin. For most of the journey, Griffin's plane was 200 miles ahead of the *Star Tiger*. The two pilots sent messages back and forth. Early on, Griffin radioed that the head winds had grown much stronger. They were blowing at 60 miles per hour. In addition, the sky had clouded up. So it would not be possible to follow the stars. Because of this, both pilots could expect to be blown somewhat off course.

7   And they were. When the skies cleared around 1:00 A.M., both planes had drifted away from their flight paths. Griffin and McMillan each made the necessary course corrections. Each now expected to be one hour late.

8   Despite the wind and the clouds, Griffin had a routine flight. At

3:00 A.M. he sent his last message to McMillan. "See you at breakfast," he said. When Griffin landed at Kindley Field, Bermuda, it was 4:11 in the morning.

9   The *Star Tiger* was expected in around 5:00 A.M. There was no reason to think it would not arrive. At 3:00 A.M., McMillan had radioed the Air Traffic Control tower in Bermuda. He had everything under control. He reported, "Weather and performance excellent."

10   At that time, McMillan was about 380 miles northeast of Bermuda. He knew his position. So, too, did the people in the control tower. Yet the *Star Tiger* never made it to Bermuda. No SOS emergency signal was ever received. The plane just disappeared.

11   When the *Star Tiger* didn't show up by 5:00 A.M., the control tower declared an emergency. A big search was launched. First, a search plane equipped with radar was sent out. When it found no trace of the missing aircraft, 25 more planes and 10 ships went looking. They covered all areas of the ocean where the plane could possibly have gone down. Bad weather

interfered with the search. Visibility was poor, and the waves were choppy. Still, the rescuers kept trying. For five days they searched. Then, sadly, they gave up. They had found nothing—no wreckage, no oil slicks, no debris, no bodies.

12 How could the *Star Tiger* simply have vanished like that? The British Ministry of Civil Aviation looked into the matter. Eight months later, its members published a report. The group had looked into all the usual causes of a plane crash. Had there been a radio failure? No, the plane carried two radios. "A total failure of radio is most unlikely," declared the report. Had there been a fire? Not likely. By 1948 fires in planes were "very rare." Could McMillan have made a mistake about his altitude? Could he have flown the plane into the sea? "There is little possibility of that," the members wrote.

13 The report also dismissed other possible causes. The plane did not run out of fuel. The *Star Tiger* did not crash because it ran into bad weather. It did not crash because of a structural defect. And it did not crash because it lost power in one of its engines. (The *Star Tiger* could have lost *two* of its four engines and still made it to Bermuda.)

14 In short, the report stated, no one could explain it. The final sentences in the report summed it up. "What happened in this case will never be known. The fate of the *Star Tiger* must forever remain an unsolved mystery."

15 The end of the *Star Tiger* was truly bizarre. But something even more bizarre happened less than a year later. On January 17, 1949, another plane from the *same* airline vanished in the *same* area. This plane was the *Star Ariel*. Twenty people were on board, including a crew of seven. The pilot's last message gave no hint of trouble. "We have reached cruising altitude. Fair weather. Expected time of arrival . . . as scheduled."

16 Once again, there was a massive search for the missing plane. And, once again, searchers found nothing at all. An investigation was held. The result was a report much like the one issued for the *Star Tiger*. This second report stated that "the cause of the accident to the *Star Ariel* is unknown."

17 The fates of the *Star Tiger* and the *Star Ariel* may never be known. But their disappearances have helped give this patch of ocean an eerie reputation. As you may have guessed, the *Star Tiger* and the *Star Ariel* disappeared in what has become known as the Bermuda Triangle.

If you have been timed while reading this article, enter your reading time below. Then turn to the Words-per-Minute Table on page 147 and look up your reading speed (words per minute). Enter your reading speed on the graph on page 148.

Reading Time: Lesson 11

———————— : ————————

Minutes   *Seconds*

A Finding the Main Idea

One statement below expresses the main idea of the article. One statement is too general, or too broad. The other statement explains only part of the article; it is too narrow. Label the statements using the following key:

M—Main Idea   **B—Too Broad**   **N—Too Narrow**

_____ 1. Some areas of the world are more dangerous for air travel than others.

_____ 2. The pilot of the *Star Tiger* first stopped at Lisbon, Portugal; after an overnight stay, he continued on toward the Azores and Bermuda.

_____ 3. The *Star Tiger* seemed to be making a routine flight to Bermuda when it suddenly vanished.

_____ Score 15 points for a correct M answer.

_____ Score 5 points for each correct B or N answer.

_____ **Total Score:** Finding the Main Idea

B Recalling Facts

How well do you remember the facts in the article? Put an X in the box next to the answer that correctly completes each statement about the article.

1. The *Star Tiger* was flying from London to
   ☐ a. New York City.
   ☐ b. Bermuda.
   ☐ c. the Bahamas.

2. Head winds are dangerous because they can
   ☐ a. blow planes off course.
   ☐ b. destroy radio communications.
   ☐ c. damage plane propellers.

3. The plane that left just before the *Star Tiger* was
   ☐ a. a cargo plane.
   ☐ b. a passenger plane.
   ☐ c. an old military plane.

4. A report on the disappearance was published by
   ☐ a. the British air force.
   ☐ b. a Bermuda transportation commission.
   ☐ c. the British Ministry of Civil Aviation.

5. The area in which the *Star Tiger* and *Star Ariel* disappeared is called the
   ☐ a. Azores.
   ☐ b. Bermuda Triangle.
   ☐ c. Tropic of Capricorn.

Score 5 points for each correct answer.

_____ **Total Score:** Recalling Facts

C Making Inferences

When you combine your own experience and information from a text to draw a conclusion that is not directly stated in that text, you are making an inference. Below are five statements that may or may not be inferences based on information in the article. Label the statements using the following key:

C—Correct Inference　　**F—Faulty Inference**

_____ 1. Today, aircraft can travel farther in a single flight than they could in 1948.

_____ 2. Only British planes ever experience difficulties during long flights over the ocean.

_____ 3. The strange disappearances of the *Star Tiger* and the *Star Ariel* were caused by the Bermuda Triangle.

_____ 4. Airplane pilots take the threat of bad weather quite seriously.

_____ 5. Pilots normally communicate regularly with control towers.

Score 5 points for each correct answer.

_____ **Total Score:** Making Inferences

D Using Words Precisely

Each numbered sentence below contains an underlined word or phrase from the article. Following the sentence are three definitions. One definition is closest to the meaning of the underlined word. One definition is opposite or nearly opposite. Label those two definitions using the following key; do not label the remaining definition.

C—Closest　　**O—Opposite or Nearly Opposite**

1. Captain Brian McMillan shook his head in <u>dismay</u>.

_____ a. relief

_____ b. disappointment

_____ c. surprise

2. So Captain McMillan, a <u>seasoned</u> pilot, knew the risks.

_____ a. bad-tempered

_____ b. new

_____ c. experienced

3. They had found nothing—no wreckage, no oil slicks, no <u>debris</u>, no bodies.

_____ a. books

_____ b. remains of something destroyed

_____ c. items in perfect condition

4. It did not crash because of a <u>structural</u> defect.

_____ a. design

_____ b. engine

_____ c. performance

5. But their disappearances have helped give this patch of ocean an <u>eerie</u> reputation.

_____ a. familiar and comforting

_____ b. spooky

_____ c. amusing

_____ Score 3 points for each correct C answer.

_____ Score 2 points for each correct O answer.

_____ **Total Score:** Using Words Precisely

Enter the four total scores in the spaces below, and add them together to find your Reading Comprehension Score. Then record your score on the graph on page 149.

Score	Question Type	Lesson 11
_____	Finding the Main Idea	
_____	Recalling Facts	
_____	Making Inferences	
_____	Using Words Precisely	
_____	**Reading Comprehension Score**	

Author's Approach

Put an X in the box next to the correct answer.

1. The main purpose of the first paragraph is to

☐ a. inform the reader about weather forecasting in the 1940s.

☐ b. describe Captain McMillan's personality.

☐ c. tell about the problem that Captain McMillan faced.

2. From the statements below, choose those that you believe the authors would agree with.

☐ a. No one knows the reason why the *Star Tiger* disappeared.

☐ b. The captain of the *Star Tiger* was a careful pilot.

☐ c. Someone probably knows but is covering up the real reason why *Star Tiger* disappeared.

3. How is the authors' purpose for writing the article expressed in paragraph 17?

☐ a. The authors stress that these plane crashes were tragic.

☐ b. The authors suggest that these plane crashes support the theory that the Bermuda Triangle is a strange place.

☐ c. The authors believe that plane crashes are unusual and newsworthy.

4. The authors tell this story mainly by

☐ a. comparing different topics.

☐ b. using their imagination and creativity.

☐ c. telling different stories about the same topic.

_____ Number of correct answers

Record your personal assessment of your work on the Critical Thinking Chart on page 150.

CRITICAL THINKING

Summarizing and Paraphrasing

Follow the directions provided for questions 1 and 2. Put an X in the box next to the correct answer for question 3.

1. Look for the important ideas and events in paragraphs 9 and 10. Summarize those paragraphs in one or two sentences.

_____

_____

_____

2. Complete the following one-sentence summary of the article using the lettered phrases from the phrase bank below. Write the letters on the lines.

Phrase Bank

a. possible reasons for the *Star Tiger's* disappearance and why they were discarded

b. the events that led to the *Star Tiger's* disappearance

c. the story of the disappearance of the *Star Ariel*

The article "The Last Flight of the *Star Tiger*" begins with

_____, goes on to explain _____, and ends with

_____.

3. Choose the best one-sentence paraphrase for the following sentence from the article: "The *Star Tiger* could have lost two of its four engines and still made it to Bermuda."

☐ a. If the *Star Tiger* had lost two of its four engines, the other two could still have taken it to Bermuda safely.

☐ b. Even though the *Star Tiger* lost two of its engines, it landed in Bermuda safely.

☐ c. The *Star Tiger* probably lost two of its engines; for that reason, it did not make it to Bermuda.

_____ Number of correct answers

Record your personal assessment of your work on the Critical Thinking Chart on page 150.

Critical Thinking

Put an X in the box next to the correct answer for questions 1, 3, and 4. Follow the directions provided for question 2.

1. From the information in paragraph 15, you can predict that

☐ a. pilots from that airline refused to fly into the Bermuda Triangle ever again.

☐ b. pilots from that airline were a little nervous when flying into the Bermuda Triangle.

☐ c. many more planes from that airline would be lost in the Bermuda Triangle.

2. Using what you know about the *Star Tiger* and what is told about the *Star Ariel* in the article, name three ways the *Star Tiger* is similar to and three ways the *Star Tiger* is different from the *Star Ariel*. Cite the paragraph number(s) where you found details in the article to support your conclusions.

Similarities

_____

_____

_____

Differences

_____

_____

_____

3. What was the effect of the disappearance of the *Star Tiger*?

☐ a. Captain Frank Griffin's plane arrived safely in Bermuda.

☐ b. The *Star Ariel* crashed in the same area one year later.

☐ c. A massive search for the *Star Tiger* was launched.

4. What did you have to do to answer question 2?

☐ a. find an opinion (what someone thinks about something)

☐ b. find a contrast (how things are different)

☐ c. draw a conclusion (a sensible statement based on the text and your experience)

_____ Number of correct answers

Record your personal assessment of your work on the Critical Thinking Chart on page 150.

Personal Response

Would you recommend this article to other students? Explain.

_____

_____

_____

Self-Assessment

The part I found most difficult about the article was _____

_____

I found this difficult because _____

_____

_____

The Tragic Donner Party

THE

EMIGRANTS' GUIDE,

TO

OREGON AND CALIFORNIA,

CONTAINING SCENES AND INCIDENTS OF A PARTY OF
OREGON EMIGRANTS;

A DESCRIPTION OF OREGON;

SCENES AND INCIDENTS OF A PARTY OF CALIFORNIA
EMIGRANTS;

AND

A DESCRIPTION OF CALIFORNIA;

WITH

A DESCRIPTION OF THE DIFFERENT ROUTES TO
THOSE COUNTRIES;

AND

ALL NECESSARY INFORMATION RELATIVE TO THE
EQUIPMENT, SUPPLIES, AND THE METHOD
OF TRAVELING.

BY LANSFORD W. HASTINGS,
Leader of the Oregon and California Emigrants of 1842.

APPLEWOOD BOOKS
BEDFORD, MASSACHUSETTS

George and Jacob Donner couldn't wait to get started. They wanted to go to California and soak up the warm sun. Both men had worked hard all their lives. Now, in 1846, they were ready to move their families away from Illinois and its harsh winters. They had plenty of money. Once they got to California, they planned to relax and live out their days in comfort.

Lansford Hastings, in his book The Emigrants' Guide to Oregon and California, *suggested that travelers on their way to the West should take a shortcut through the Sierra Nevada mountains. Unfortunately, the Donner party followed his advice to the letter.*

2   The Donner brothers knew the trip west would be long and hard. They would have to travel more than 2,000 miles in ox-drawn wagons. But the Donners weren't worried. They had a book that told them how to do it. It was called *The Emigrants' Guide to Oregon and California*. The author was Lansford Hastings.

3   According to Hastings, California was a paradise. It had beautiful weather all year long. As Hastings knew, most people got to California by following the Oregon Trail. That took them west to Fort Bridger in what is now Wyoming. From there, the trail looped north to Oregon, then down to California. Hastings, however, claimed he knew a better way. He advised people not to turn north at Fort Bridger. Instead, he said, they should keep going straight west. He said there was a trail there that would take them right through the mountains of the Sierra Nevada.

4   Hastings's shortcut sounded good. George and Jacob Donner planned to use it. They didn't know that Hastings had left out one fact. The "shortcut" had not yet been cut.

It existed only in Hastings's imagination.

5   In April of 1846 the Donners packed up and headed west. They joined other pioneers on the westward trek. Together, these families formed a great wagon train.

6   At first, the trail was smooth and easy to follow. Folks gathered around the campfire at night to tell stories and sing songs. They held open-air church services. The women formed sewing circles. And the children had dozens of playmates.

7   Soon, though, things became more difficult. The early sense of adventure gave way to boredom. The trail seemed endless. The sun beat down without mercy. As the wagon train headed up into the Rockies, the ground became hard and rutted, and grass for the animals grew scarce. People lost their temper. Quarrels—even fistfights— broke out. Soon the great wagon train split up into several smaller ones.

8   About this time, the Donners' wagon train met a man named James Clyman. He was a grubby-looking wanderer who had already been to California. Now he was heading back

east. Clyman said he had tried to use Hastings's shortcut. He warned everyone that it was sheer wilderness. He advised people to stay on the Oregon Trail.

9   Some people heeded Clyman's warning. They took the safer route. But the Donners believed in Hastings. They ignored Clyman's advice. Several other families did, too. In all, 87 people chose the shortcut. They elected George Donner to be their captain.

10   By July 31 the Donner party had reached Fort Bridger. They split off from the Oregon Trail and headed straight for the Sierra Nevada. But one thing after another slowed them down. A young boy fell off a horse and needed care. The party took some wrong turns into blind canyons and had to backtrack to get out. The Donner party hoped for better luck as their wagons neared the Great Salt Lake valley. But here they had to hack their way through deep underbrush. It took them 16 days to travel just 36 miles.

11   Next came the Great Salt Desert. Hastings had written that it could be

crossed in just one day. But it really took six days. George Donner and the others realized they would never make it unless they lightened their load. They left many of their wagons, loaded with possessions, to rot in the desert.

12   The Donner party was falling further and further behind schedule. It was already September. The weather was turning colder. Nonetheless, they had to keep going—they had come too far to turn back. They could only hope that winter would arrive late.

13   As the days grew shorter, people's moods grew worse. One man was killed in a knife fight. Another was secretly murdered. An elderly member fell behind, and nobody bothered to look for him.

14   But then, for a moment, things looked brighter. Two members of the Donner party had gone ahead to get help. On October 19 one of them returned with two Indian guides. This man brought food. He also brought news that the mountains were still passable. The snows had not yet come.

15   The Donner party rested for a few days in preparation for the climb through the Sierras. It would be the greatest challenge of the whole journey. The travelers would have to scale huge walls of rock and scramble over enormous boulders. It was the last hurdle they faced. If they could get over the mountains, they would be all right.

16   Soon after they began the climb, however, they found the pass blocked with five feet of fresh snow. They struggled to keep going but finally had to turn back. They set up camp at what is now called Donner Lake. In a day or two, they thought, they would have the energy to push on.

17   But the next morning they woke up half-buried in snow. It kept snowing for the next eight days. Now they were trapped. All they could do was settle down by the lake and wait for spring.

18   Using logs and some canvas from the wagons, they built rough shelters. The shelters helped to keep them warm. But hunger was a terrible problem. After eating what little food they had, they killed and ate their animals. Next they boiled animal hides to make soup. Finally, they started eating field mice, even tree bark.

19   By early December, things looked hopeless. In a last-ditch effort at survival, 17 people agreed to go for help. They made crude snowshoes and packed up a few mouthfuls of food. Then they headed off over the mountains. For 33 days they walked through the snow. They suffered unspeakable hardships. When the group finally crawled down the other side of the mountains, only seven were still alive. Those seven had survived by cooking and eating the flesh of those who died.

20   Alerted to the situation, rescuers headed for Donner Lake. They arrived on February 18. As they approached the campsite, they saw nothing. Had everyone died? One rescuer gave a shout. Slowly, half-human shapes emerged from under a deep cover of snow. Some people had survived the winter. They had done it the same way the snowshoers did. They had eaten the bodies of those who died.

21   Thirty-five members of the Donner party died in the mountains. These pioneers had come west for the warmth and sun of California. But in a cruel twist of fate, California's cold and snow had ended their lives.

If you have been timed while reading this article, enter your reading time below. Then turn to the Words-per-Minute Table on page 147 and look up your reading speed (words per minute). Enter your reading speed on the graph on page 148.

Reading Time: Lesson 12

——————— : ———————
Minutes   Seconds

A Finding the Main Idea

One statement below expresses the main idea of the article. One statement is too general, or too broad. The other statement explains only part of the article; it is too narrow. Label the statements using the following key:

M—Main Idea   **B—Too Broad**   **N—Too Narrow**

_____ 1. It took the Donner party six days to cross the Great Salt Desert instead of the one day that their guidebook promised.

_____ 2. Because they trusted a poor guidebook, the Donner party traveled west slowly and was trapped by snow in the mountains, where most of its members died.

_____ 3. The pioneers who traveled across the American prairies during the 1800s faced many dreadful dangers.

_____ Score 15 points for a correct M answer.

_____ Score 5 points for each correct B or N answer.

_____ **Total Score:** Finding the Main Idea

B Recalling Facts

How well do you remember the facts in the article? Put an X in the box next to the answer that correctly completes each statement about the article.

1. George and Jacob Donner began their trip in
   ☐ a. New England.
   ☐ b. Illinois.
   ☐ c. 1929.

2. To get to California, the Donners relied on
   ☐ a. a compass and stories they had heard.
   ☐ b. an experienced guide, Lansford Hastings.
   ☐ c. a guidebook by Lansford Hastings.

3. Most pioneers turned north at Fort Bridger
   ☐ a. to tell stories and sing songs.
   ☐ b. because they were bound for Oregon.
   ☐ c. to avoid crossing the Sierra Nevada.

4. James Clyman advised the Donners
   ☐ a. to stay on the Oregon Trail.
   ☐ b. that native tribes would attack soon.
   ☐ c. to take additional water across the desert.

5. Some of the Donner party survived by
   ☐ a. building warm houses of stone.
   ☐ b. eating the flesh of those who died.
   ☐ c. trading with Indians for food.

Score 5 points for each correct answer.

_____ **Total Score:** Recalling Facts

C Making Inferences

When you combine your own experience and information from a text to draw a conclusion that is not directly stated in that text, you are making an inference. Below are five statements that may or may not be inferences based on information in the article. Label the statements using the following key:

C—Correct Inference   **F—Faulty Inference**

_____ 1. The author Lansford Hastings was at least partly responsible for the disaster of the Donner party.

_____ 2. Every westbound group was as poorly directed as the Donner party.

_____ 3. The fact that the members of the Donner party did not get along well contributed to the disaster.

_____ 4. Later travelers found possessions of the Donner party in the Great Salt Desert.

_____ 5. All the pioneers really needed to make the westward journey safely was an accurate map, plenty of food for their families, and weapons for defense.

Score 5 points for each correct answer.

_____ **Total Score:** Making Inferences

D Using Words Precisely

Each numbered sentence below contains an underlined word or phrase from the article. Following the sentence are three definitions. One definition is closest to the meaning of the underlined word. One definition is opposite or nearly opposite. Label those two definitions using the following key; do not label the remaining definition.

C—Closest   **O—Opposite or Nearly Opposite**

1. It was called *The Emigrants' Guide to Oregon and California*. The author was Lansford Hastings.

_____ a. people who move into a country

_____ b. people who move out of a country

_____ c. people who fight against their government

2. According to Hastings, California was a paradise.

_____ a. desert

_____ b. pain-filled place to be avoided

_____ c. place of unlimited joys

3. He was a grubby-looking wanderer who had already been to California.

_____ a. dirty

_____ b. clean

_____ c. dishonest

4. The party took some wrong turns into blind canyons and had to backtrack to get out.

_____ a. very narrow

_____ b. closed at one end

_____ c. free from obstacles; clear; open

5. The travelers would have to <u>scale</u> huge walls of rock and scramble over enormous boulders.

_____ a. descend; come down

_____ b. smash through

_____ c. climb up

_____ Score 3 points for each correct C answer.

_____ Score 2 points for each correct O answer.

_____ **Total Score:** Using Words Precisely

Enter the four total scores in the spaces below, and add them together to find your Reading Comprehension Score. Then record your score on the graph on page 149.

Score	Question Type	Lesson 12
_____	Finding the Main Idea	
_____	Recalling Facts	
_____	Making Inferences	
_____	Using Words Precisely	
_____	**Reading Comprehension Score**	

Author's Approach

Put an X in the box next to the correct answer.

1. What does the author mean by the statement "Some people heeded Clyman's warning. They took the safer route"?

☐ a. Some people believed Clyman and took the Oregon Trail instead of the one that Hastings recommended.

☐ b. Some people became afraid and headed back east.

☐ c. Some people listened to Clyman and took the Santa Fe Trail west.

2. The main purpose of the first paragraph is to

☐ a. explain why the Donner brothers were traveling west.

☐ b. compare Jacob and George Donner.

☐ c. describe the hardships the Donner party faced on their trip.

3. What is the authors' purpose in writing "The Tragic Donner Party"?

☐ a. to entertain readers with a pleasant story

☐ b. to inform the reader about a sad page in history

☐ c. to express an opinion about the truthfulness of Lansford Hastings

4. Which of the following statements from the article best describes the trail that Hastings recommended?

☐ a. Hastings's shortcut sounded good.

☐ b. From [Fort Bridger], the trail looped north to Oregon, then down to California.

☐ c. It existed only in Hastings's imagination.

_____ Number of correct answers

Record your personal assessment of your work on the Critical Thinking Chart on page 150.

Summarizing and Paraphrasing

Follow the directions provided for questions 1 and 3. Put an X in the box next to the correct answer for question 2.

1. Complete the following one-sentence summary of the article using the lettered phrases from the phrase bank below. Write the letters on the lines.

> ### Phrase Bank
> a. difficulties the party faced
> b. the Donner brothers' plans for the future
> c. the rescue of the survivors

The article "The Tragic Donner Party" begins with _____,

goes on to explain _____, and ends with _____.

2. Below are summaries of the article. Choose the summary that says all the most important things about the article, but in the fewest words.

☐ a. Pioneers in the Donner party followed the trail recommended by Lansford Hastings in his book, *The Emigrants' Guide to Oregon and California,* and they found themselves trapped in the Sierra Nevada Mountains for much of the winter of 1846–1847.

☐ b. Because they followed the trail recommended in Lansford Hastings's book, the Donner party faced incredible hardships. They were trapped in the Sierra Nevada mountains, and many starved to death before rescuers came.

☐ c. Many bad decisions and personal problems kept the Donner party from reaching California.

3. Reread paragraph 12 in the article. Below, write a summary of the paragraph in no more than 25 words.

_____

_____

_____

_____

Reread your summary and decide whether it covers the important ideas in the paragraph. Next, decide how to shorten the summary to 15 words or less without leaving out any essential information. Write this summary below.

_____

_____

_____

_____ Number of correct answers

Record your personal assessment of your work on the Critical Thinking Chart on page 150.

Critical Thinking

Follow the directions provided for questions 1, 3, and 4. Put an X in the box next to the correct answer for question 2.

1. For each statement below, write *O* if it expresses an opinion or write *F* if it expresses a fact.

   _____ a. In April of 1846 the Donners packed up and headed west.

   _____ b. At first the trail was smooth and easy to follow.

   _____ c. The members of the party who snowshoed over the mountains were braver than the ones who stayed behind in the camp.

2. From what the article told about the trail recommended in Hastings's book, you can predict that survivors

   ☐ a. recommended that trail to other pioneers.

   ☐ b. felt sorry for Hastings because they knew he had tried hard to find a good trail.

   ☐ c. advised everyone not to follow that trail.

3. Choose from the letters below to correctly complete the following statement. Write the letters on the lines.

   In the article, _____ and _____ are different.

   a. the Oregon Trail

   b. the trail that Hastings recommended

   c. the trail that the Donner party followed

4. Reread paragraph 17. Then choose from the letters below to correctly complete the following statement. Write the letters on the lines.

   According to paragraph 17, _____ because _____.

   a. it snowed one night

   b. snow kept falling for days

   c. the Donner party became trapped in the mountains

_____ Number of correct answers

Record your personal assessment of your work on the Critical Thinking Chart on page 150.

Personal Response

What new question do you have about this topic?

_____

_____

_____

_____

Self-Assessment

I can't really understand how _____

_____

_____

_____

Courage in the Face of Evil

William Boyd remembers the last time he saw Ken Saro-Wiwa. It was in England in 1992. Saro-Wiwa was on his way back to his home in Nigeria. Boyd shook Saro-Wiwa's hand and said goodbye. "Be careful, Ken," he told him. "OK?"

2   Saro-Wiwa smiled at his friend. "Oh, I'll be very careful," he replied. "Don't worry." But in his gut, Boyd feared Saro-Wiwa was headed for trouble.

3   In many ways, Ken Saro-Wiwa had it made. He had money, friends, and

The Ogoni, who live near the banks of the Niger River in Nigeria, Africa, have had to endure their new neighbors, the oil companies, who have polluted the water, land, and air. Writer Ken Saro-Wiwa spoke up for his people—and for the environment.

talent. He owned a home in England where his wife and four children lived. He had a place in his native Nigeria too. There, Saro-Wiwa was a hero. The Nigerian people loved him. He had written many books. One was a best-selling novel about the country's bloody civil war. Saro-Wiwa also produced a hit TV show called *Basi and Co.* It was a smart, funny program.

4   So what made William Boyd worry about his friend? Over the past few years, Saro-Wiwa had taken on a dangerous fight. He had been trying to call attention to the plight of his people, the Ogoni. The Ogoni are one of 250 ethnic groups in Nigeria. There are about 500,000 Ogoni living along the Niger River. Most are dirt poor. But their lands contain vast riches in the form of oil deposits.

5   In 1958, oil companies moved onto Ogoni land and began drilling for oil. The Ogoni objected. They felt the oil belonged to them. If money was being made off it, they wanted a fair share of the profits. In fact, the oil companies were making billions of dollars. But none of that money was going to the Ogoni. Instead, the oil companies split

their profits with Nigeria's corrupt rulers.

6   The Ogoni felt robbed. But that wasn't the worst of it. Oil drilling was ruining their land and water. Most Ogoni earned their living by farming and fishing. But now oil began spilling out of leaky pipelines. The soil turned black and greasy. Fishing grounds also became polluted. The air was filled with black smoke from oil fires, and acid rain fell on the trees.

7   Ken Saro-Wiwa wanted to change things. He wanted the oil companies to clean up the mess they had made. In 1990 he formed a group called MOSOP (Movement for the Survival of the Ogoni People). As head of the group, Ken Saro-Wiwa made his voice heard. He set up marches. He wrote letters and gave speeches.

8   His methods were nonviolent. Still, he angered some people. Rich Nigerians liked things just the way they were. So did the country's brutal ruler, General Sani Abacha. The oil companies, too, did not want to be bothered with clean-up efforts. With so many enemies, it is no wonder Saro-Wiwa often ended up in jail. After spending a few weeks or

months behind bars, he would be freed. But it was clear that Abacha and others wished to be rid of him once and for all.

9   Their chance came on May 21, 1994. A rally was held in the town of Giokoo. It was organized by MOSOP. But the rally was led by members who disagreed with Saro-Wiwa's methods. Saro-Wiwa wanted to go to the rally anyway. He wanted to speak to these members and explain to them why his way was better. But the road to Giokoo was blocked by army trucks. So Saro-Wiwa drove back home. The rally took place without him. During it, a riot broke out. Four people were killed in the bloody chaos.

10   General Abacha did not hesitate. He sent troops to arrest Saro-Wiwa. The charge? At first, there was none. The army just kept Saro-Wiwa in prison. Then, after a year, Abacha announced his plan. He would charge Saro-Wiwa with murder. It was an outrageous charge. Saro-Wiwa had not killed anyone at the rally. He hadn't even been there. But that detail did not bother Abacha. He claimed Saro-Wiwa had stirred people up and incited them to kill.

11   People around the world flooded Abacha with protests. They were dismayed by his actions. But he didn't care. He just wanted to get rid of Saro-Wiwa. He ordered Saro-Wiwa brought

to trial—but not in a real court. Instead, Saro-Wiwa would be tried by a special army court. The three "judges" would be handpicked by the army. And Saro-Wiwa would have no right of appeal.

12   The court found Saro-Wiwa guilty. (Two witnesses later admitted that they had been paid to lie.) He was sentenced to death by hanging. The rest of the world was appalled. Saro-Wiwa was one of the most noble men of the 20th century. In fact, while in jail, he was awarded the 1995 Goldman Prize, which is given each year to someone who fights to save the environment.

13   Saro-Wiwa could not accept the Goldman Prize in person. But a note was smuggled out of his jail cell. The note was read by his son, Ken, Jr., at the award ceremony. "The environment," wrote Saro-Wiwa, "is man's first fight. Without a safe environment, man cannot exist to claim other rights." Saro-Wiwa asked the world to "stand by me and the Ogoni people."

14   After the death sentence was announced, many people turned to the oil companies. Couldn't they do something to save Saro-Wiwa? "No," said Shell Oil Company, the largest driller. "It would be dangerous and wrong" to interfere in the matter. The company said it would not meddle in a country's "legal processes."

15   Ken Saro-Wiwa faced death with great courage. William Boyd called him "the bravest man I have known." As Saro-Wiwa prepared to die, he held on to his faith in the future. He believed his work would not be in vain. In a letter smuggled out to Boyd, he wrote, "I'm in good spirits. . . . There's no doubt that my idea will succeed in time. . . . I think I have the moral victory."

16   Many people clung to the hope that General Abacha would back down. But appeals for justice meant nothing to Abacha. He didn't care what the rest of the world thought of him. On November 10, 1995, he ordered the execution to take place. Ken Saro-Wiwa was taken to the gallows and hanged. When he was pronounced dead, people around the world sobbed openly. The world had lost a great leader and a great man.

If you have been timed while reading this article, enter your reading time below. Then turn to the Words-per-Minute Table on page 147 and look up your reading speed (words per minute). Enter your reading speed on the graph on page 148.

Reading Time: Lesson 13

_____ : _____
Minutes   Seconds

A | Finding the Main Idea

One statement below expresses the main idea of the article. One statement is too general, or too broad. The other statement explains only part of the article; it is too narrow. Label the statements using the following key:

M—Main Idea   **B—Too Broad**   **N—Too Narrow**

_____ 1. Ken Saro-Wiwa was a hero because he defended the environment in spite of personal danger.

_____ 2. The environment must be protected or else all life on Earth is threatened.

_____ 3. In 1995 Ken Saro-Wiwa won the Goldman Prize for those who fight to save the environment.

_____ Score 15 points for a correct M answer.

_____ Score 5 points for each correct B or N answer.

_____ **Total Score:** Finding the Main Idea

B | Recalling Facts

How well do you remember the facts in the article? Put an X in the box next to the answer that correctly completes each statement about the article.

1. Ken Saro-Wiwa was a native of
   ☐ a. England.
   ☐ b. Nigeria.
   ☐ c. Japan.

2. The Ogoni lands are rich in
   ☐ a. oil deposits.
   ☐ b. gold.
   ☐ c. iron ore.

3. Saro-Wiwa was arrested after MOSOP held a bloody rally in
   ☐ a. Giokoo.
   ☐ b. Abacha.
   ☐ c. England.

4. Saro-Wiwa was convicted of
   ☐ a. treason.
   ☐ b. robbery.
   ☐ c. murder.

5. Saro-Wiwa could not accept his Goldman Prize in person because he was
   ☐ a. too ill to attend the ceremony.
   ☐ b. in jail.
   ☐ c. in hiding.

Score 5 points for each correct answer.

_____ **Total Score:** Recalling Facts

C | Making Inferences

When you combine your own experience and information from a text to draw a conclusion that is not directly stated in that text, you are making an inference. Below are five statements that may or may not be inferences based on information in the article. Label the statements using the following key:

C—Correct Inference   F—Faulty Inference

_____ 1. Ken Saro-Wiwa began his fight for the environment in order to become famous and rich.

_____ 2. The next winners of the Goldman Prize will probably be the oil companies drilling in Nigeria.

_____ · 3. It is dangerous to oppose powerful and wealthy people and organizations.

_____ 4. In Nigeria people can be arrested and held in jail without being charged with a crime.

_____ 5. If the United States had protested before Saro-Wiwa's execution, it would not have taken place.

Score 5 points for each correct answer.

_____ **Total Score:** Making Inferences

D | Using Words Precisely

Each numbered sentence below contains an underlined word or phrase from the article. Following the sentence are three definitions. One definition is closest to the meaning of the underlined word. One definition is opposite or nearly opposite. Label those two definitions using the following key; do not label the remaining definition.

C—Closest   O—Opposite or Nearly Opposite

1. He had been trying to call attention to the <u>plight</u> of his people, the Ogoni.

_____ a. comfortable condition

_____ b. bad situation

_____ c. history

2. Four people were killed in the bloody <u>chaos</u>.

_____ a. battle

_____ b. peace and order

_____ c. confusion and disorder

3. He claimed Saro-Wiwa had stirred people up and <u>incited</u> them to kill.

_____ a. urged; inspired

_____ b. taught

_____ c. discouraged

4. The rest of the world was <u>appalled</u>.

_____ a. shocked; dismayed

_____ b. pleased

_____ c. interested

5. The company said it would not <u>meddle</u> in a country's "legal processes."

_____ a. ignore

_____ b. interfere

_____ c. rejoice

_____ Score 3 points for each correct C answer.

_____ Score 2 points for each correct O answer.

_____ **Total Score:** Using Words Precisely

Enter the four total scores in the spaces below, and add them together to find your Reading Comprehension Score. Then record your score on the graph on page 149.

Score	Question Type	Lesson 13
_____	Finding the Main Idea	
_____	Recalling Facts	
_____	Making Inferences	
_____	Using Words Precisely	
_____	**Reading Comprehension Score**	

Author's Approach

Put an X in the box next to the correct answer.

1. The authors use the first sentence of the article to

☐ a. describe Ken Saro-Wiwa.

☐ b. suggest that something bad might happen to Ken Saro-Wiwa.

☐ c. compare William Boyd and Ken Saro-Wiwa.

2. What do the authors mean by the statement "But in his gut, Boyd feared Saro-Wiwa was headed for trouble"?

☐ a. Boyd was afraid of Saro-Wiwa.

☐ b. Boyd was angry with Saro-Wiwa for his recklessness.

☐ c. Deep down, Boyd was afraid that what Saro-Wiwa was doing would bring trouble.

3. What is the authors' purpose in writing "Courage in the Face of Evil"?

☐ a. to encourage the reader to protest the killing of Ken Saro-Wiwa

☐ b. to inform the reader about a great man who was killed

☐ c. to persuade people to care for the environment

4. The authors tell this story mainly by

☐ a. telling about events in the order they happened.

☐ b. comparing different topics.

☐ c. using their imagination and creativity.

_____ Number of correct answers

Record your personal assessment of your work on the Critical Thinking Chart on page 150.

Summarizing and Paraphrasing

Follow the directions provided for question 1. Put an X in the box next to the correct answer for the other questions.

1. Look for the important ideas and events in paragraphs 11 and 12. Summarize those paragraphs in one or two sentences.

_____

_____

_____

2. Below are summaries of the article. Choose the summary that says all the most important things about the article but in the fewest words.

☐ a.   In spite of protests from around the world, Ken Saro-Wiwa was unfairly arrested, tried, and hanged for murder. He had not even been near the scene of the crime.

☐ b.   Ken Saro-Wiwa was a member of the Ogoni tribe of Nigeria. His tribe was angry because oil companies were polluting the Ogoni land and making huge profits at the same time.

☐ c.   Ken Saro-Wiwa was a Nigerian writer who dared to disagree with his government about crimes against the environment. In 1994 he was unfairly arrested, tried, and hanged for his efforts while the world protested.

3. Choose the sentence that correctly restates the following sentence from the article: "Saro-Wiwa could not accept the Goldman Prize in person."

☐ a.   Saro-Wiwa said he could never accept the Goldman Prize.

☐ b.   Saro-Wiwa was not able to travel to the Goldman Prize awards ceremony.

☐ c.   The Goldman Prize could not be awarded just to Saro-Wiwa alone.

_____ Number of correct answers

Record your personal assessment of your work on the Critical Thinking Chart on page 150.

Critical Thinking

Put an X in the box next to the correct answer for questions 1, 2, 4, and 5. Follow the directions provided for question 3.

1. Which of the following statements from the article is an opinion rather than a fact?

☐ a.   In 1958, oil companies moved onto Ogoni land and began drilling for oil.

☐ b.   Four people were killed in the bloody chaos.

☐ c.   In many ways, Ken Saro-Wiwa had it made.

2. Judging by the events in the article, you can predict that the following will happen next:

☐ a. Abacha will feel relieved to have finally gotten rid of Saro-Wiwa.

☐ b. Abacha will deeply regret what he has done.

☐ c. Abacha will have a change of heart and start fighting to protect the environment against the oil companies.

3. Choose from the letters below to correctly complete the following statement. Write the letters on the lines.

On the positive side, _____, but on the negative side

_____.

a. Saro-Wiwa died trying to save his tribe's land and water

b. the world community learned about the pollution the oil companies were causing

c. a rally was held by MOSOP in 1994

4. How is "Courage in the Face of Evil" related to the theme of *Bizarre Endings*?

☐ a. It tells about the unfair execution of an innocent man.

☐ b. It tells about a man who got into trouble with his government.

☐ c. It tells about a man who worked to save the environment.

5. What did you have to do to answer question 2?

☐ a. find an opinion (what someone thinks about something)

☐ b. find a prediction (what might happen next)

☐ c. find a comparison (how things are the same)

_____ Number of correct answers

Record your personal assessment of your work on the Critical Thinking Chart on page 150.

Personal Response

I wonder why _____

_____

_____

_____

Self-Assessment

From reading this article, I have learned _____

_____

_____

_____

Death on Mount Everest

On the night of June 7, 1924, George Mallory and Andrew Irvine slept on the mountain alone. Their camp was at 27,000 feet. The next morning they headed for the summit of Mount Everest. At 29,028 feet Everest is the highest peak in the world. The two men had to get to the top and back before dark. If they failed they would likely die. The top of Everest is too windy and cold for anyone to be caught in the open at night.

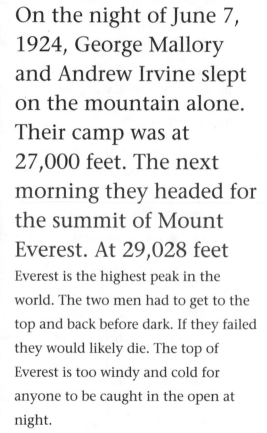

Early mountain climbers Andrew Irvine and George Mallory (standing, from left) pose with other members of the 1924 British expedition to Mount Everest. Mallory's body was found only recently, and Irvine's body was never found. The question is, Did they die going up or coming down?

2   Around 1 P.M. Noel Odell spotted the men climbing up a steep ledge. Odell was a member of Mallory's team. But he was so far down the mountain that, to him, the climbers looked like black dots. Still, he said they were "going strong for the top." Odell later said Mallory and Irvine were only 800 feet from the summit. Then they disappeared into a thick cloud. Odell never saw them again. Neither did anyone else.

3   Before the climb Mallory had a spooky feeling that something might go wrong. In fact he almost didn't climb at all. When the British Alpine Club asked him to help lead an eight-man expedition, he paused. Although he was a fine climber, he was getting older. Also, he was married and had three small children.

4   In the end, however, the 37-year-old adventurer agreed. At that time no one had ever made it to the top of Mount Everest. The dream of being the first to stand on the world's highest summit was too powerful to resist. Mallory knew the risks. He knew he might die. So he had no false hopes. "This is going to be more like war than mountaineering," he told a friend. "I don't expect to come back."

5   Mallory and Irvine died near the summit. There was no doubt about that. But they left two intriguing questions. How did they die? Did they make it to the top? For a long time it seemed as if the world would never know the answer to either question.

6   Later, other climbers conquered Mount Everest. Edmund Hillary and Tenzing Norgay reached the top in 1954. Since then more than 1,000 climbers have made the trip. High-tech equipment and clothing have made the ascent easier. Still, it remains a hard and often deadly climb. Over the years about 150 people have died on Everest.

7   Although Mallory and Irvine were gone, they were not forgotten. Many climbers thought of them as heroes. After all, they gave up their lives trying to go where no human had ever gone before. And people still debated whether they had reached the summit. If they had, they deserved credit for being the first. But there was no way to know for sure. Their bodies had never been found.

8   People knew that Mallory had carried a camera. If someone could find his body, he or she might also find the camera. The cold mountain air might have preserved the film. So perhaps the photos could still be developed. Surely Mallory and Irvine would have taken a picture of each other if they had reached the summit. Such a photo would prove they had made it.

9   Without the bodies, however, all people could do was guess. Over the years some clues did turn up. In 1933 Irvine's ice ax was found. Then in 1975 a Chinese climber saw a frozen body lying face up in the snow. He called it "old English dead."

10   For some reason the Chinese climber kept the big news to himself for three years. At last he mentioned it to another climber. The very next day, however, the Chinese man died in an avalanche. He died before revealing the exact spot where he had seen the body.

11   Experts knew the route the Chinese climber had taken. It was west of the path most climbers used. It was in the same area where Irvine's ax had been

found. So people figured the body belonged to Irvine.

12   Still, for a long time no one went looking for it. After all, it was way up in what climbers called the Death Zone. That meant it was above 26,000 feet. There is not much oxygen at that altitude. Also, winds often top 100 miles per hour. The temperature stays well below zero. No one can live long in such conditions. Anyone who enters the Death Zone struggles to stay alive. The land is steep and slippery. Climbers know that if they make one false step, Everest will claim another victim.

13   Finally, in 1999 a climber named Eric Simonson put together a search team. He hoped to find the body of either George Mallory or Andrew Irvine. "Most people didn't think we had a prayer," he said.

14   On May 1 Simonson's team began searching in the Death Zone. It took them just 90 minutes to find a body. But it was not the one the Chinese climber had seen. That body had been face up, while this one was face down. This body was clinging to the side of a slope. The frigid air had preserved it so well that it looked like a white statue. The body had a rope tied around its waist. As the men took a closer look, one of them exclaimed, "Oh, my God. It's George!"

15   The team pried George Mallory's body off the icy ground. It took hours to do that. The team also gathered up the personal items Mallory had in his clothes. Then they buried his body under rocks. This mountain had been his grave for 74 years; there was no need to move him now.

16   Finding Mallory's body answered the question of how he died. He had fallen nearly a thousand feet. He had broken his leg and hurt his head in the fall. The broken rope around his waist proved that Irvine had been tied to him when the accident took place. Surprisingly, it seemed they must have been climbing at night. In the daytime the sun bounces off the snow with blinding brightness. Yet searchers found Mallory's sunglasses tucked away in his pocket.

17   Simonson's team concluded that the fall itself didn't kill Mallory. The body was not sprawled on the snow. Instead Mallory's hands were gripping the slope as if he was trying to climb. So he must have lived through the fall but died soon after.

18   The team did not find Irvine's body. Simonson thinks that Irvine, too, survived the fall. He probably died trying to drag himself back to camp.

19   Unfortunately the team couldn't answer the question of whether the two

men made it to the summit. Searchers didn't find the camera. Mallory had said he would place a photo of his wife on the summit. The photo wasn't found in his pockets. Had it blown off the dead body? Or had Mallory indeed left it at the summit?

20   Perhaps someday Mallory's camera will be found. Or perhaps Irvine's body will be found and will provide some clear-cut answers. But until more is learned, no one can say for sure whether Mallory and Irvine ever stood on top of the highest mountain in the world.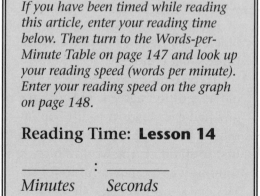

If you have been timed while reading this article, enter your reading time below. Then turn to the Words-per-Minute Table on page 147 and look up your reading speed (words per minute). Enter your reading speed on the graph on page 148.

Reading Time: Lesson 14

_____ : _____
Minutes   Seconds

A | Finding the Main Idea

One statement below expresses the main idea of the article. One statement is too general, or too broad. The other statement explains only part of the article; it is too narrow. Label the statements using the following key:

M—Main Idea   **B—Too Broad**   **N—Too Narrow**

_____ 1. The mystery of which climbers were the first to reach the top of Mount Everest has not yet been solved.

_____ 2. In 1999 a Mount Everest search party found the body of legendary climber George Mallory. Experts are still not sure whether Mallory and his partner, Andrew Irvine, were the first to reach the top.

_____ 3. George Mallory, a 37-year-old mountain climber who attempted to climb Mount Everest, must have died after a terrible fall while he was tied to his partner, Andrew Irvine.

_____ Score 15 points for a correct M answer.

_____ Score 5 points for each correct B or N answer.

_____ **Total Score:** Finding the Main Idea

B | Recalling Facts

How well do you remember the facts in the article? Put an X in the box next to the answer that correctly completes each statement about the article.

1. George Mallory and Andrew Irvine tried to climb Mount Everest in
   ☐ a. June 1924.
   ☐ b. October 1924.
   ☐ c. August 1924.

2. Climbers call the area above 26,000 feet
   ☐ a. Dead Man's Peak.
   ☐ b. No Man's Land.
   ☐ c. the Death Zone.

3. In 1999 George Mallory's body was found by a search team led by
   ☐ a. a Chinese climber who soon died in an avalanche.
   ☐ b. Andrew Irvine.
   ☐ c. Eric Simonson.

4. George Mallory had died as a result of a fall that broke his
   ☐ a. arm and his leg.
   ☐ b. leg and injured his head.
   ☐ c. back.

5. The item that the search team was most disappointed not to find was Mallory's
   ☐ a. oxygen tank.
   ☐ b. camera.
   ☐ c. journal.

Score 5 points for each correct answer.

_____ **Total Score:** Recalling Facts

C Making Inferences

When you combine your own experience with information from a text to draw a conclusion that is not directly stated in that text, you are making an inference. Below are five statements that may or may not be inferences based on information in the article. Label the statements using the following key:

C—Correct Inference   **F—Faulty Inference**

_____ 1. The weather on Mount Everest causes a human body to rot very quickly.

_____ 2. The two climbers trusted each other.

_____ 3. Unusually bad weather was probably responsible for the deaths of the two climbers.

_____ 4. Some camera film may be able to withstand very cold temperatures.

_____ 5. Nighttime is probably the best time to climb a mountain.

Score 5 points for each correct answer.

_____ **Total Score:** Making Inferences

D Using Words Precisely

Each numbered sentence below contains an underlined word or phrase from the article. Following the sentence are three definitions. One definition is closest to the meaning of the underlined word. One definition is opposite or nearly opposite. Label those two definitions using the following key; do not label the remaining definition.

C—Closest   **O—Opposite or Nearly Opposite**

1. But they left two <u>intriguing</u> questions.

_____ a. boring

_____ b. fascinating

_____ c. difficult

2. High-tech equipment and clothing have made the <u>ascent</u> easier.

_____ a. trip up

_____ b. sport

_____ c. climb down

3. And people still <u>debated</u> whether they had reached the summit.

_____ a. doubted

_____ b. agreed about

_____ c. argued about

4. The body was not <u>sprawled</u> on the snow.

_____ a. injured

_____ b. lying with legs and arms spread out

_____ c. rolled up in a tight ball

5. Instead, Mallory's hands were <u>gripping</u> the slope as if he was trying to climb.

_____ a. letting go of

_____ b. pointing to

_____ c. holding onto

_____ Score 3 points for each correct C answer.

_____ Score 2 points for each correct O answer.

_____ **Total Score:** Using Words Precisely

Enter the four total scores in the spaces below, and add them together to find your Reading Comprehension Score. Then record your score on the graph on page 149.

Score	Question Type	Lesson 14
_____	Finding the Main Idea	
_____	Recalling Facts	
_____	Making Inferences	
_____	Using Words Precisely	
_____	**Reading Comprehension Score**	

Author's Approach

Put an X in the box next to the correct answer.

1. The main purpose of the first paragraph is to

☐ a. describe the friendship between George Mallory and Andrew Irvine.

☐ b. create a mood of suspense.

☐ c. compare George Mallory and Andrew Irvine.

2. Which of the following statements from the article best describes the reason that Mallory decided to lead the expedition?

☐ a. Before the climb Mallory had a spooky feeling that something might go wrong.

☐ b. Although he was a fine climber, he was getting older.

☐ c. The dream of being the first to stand on the world's highest summit was too powerful to resist.

3. From the statements below, choose those that you believe the authors would agree with.

☐ a. It will be interesting to find out who really climbed Mount Everest first.

☐ b. People should stop searching for Mallory's camera, since the search itself is too risky.

☐ c. People will probably keep on looking for Mallory's camera, since they want to solve this mystery.

_____ Number of correct answers

Record your personal assessment of your work on the Critical Thinking Chart on page 150.

Summarizing and Paraphrasing

Follow the directions provided for questions 1 and 2. Put an X in the box next to the correct answer for question 3.

1. Look for the important ideas and events in paragraphs 9 and 10. Summarize those paragraphs in one or two sentences.

_____

_____

_____

2. Complete the following one-sentence summary of the article using the lettered phrases from the phrase bank below. Write the letters on the lines.

Phrase Bank

a. why people were interested in finding Mallory and Irvine's bodies

b. the story of Mallory and Irvine's ascent and death on the mountain

c. the findings of the Simonson expedition

The article "Death on Mount Everest" begins with _____,

goes on to explain _____, and ends with _____.

3. Choose the best one-sentence paraphrase for the following sentence from the article: "Most people didn't think we had a prayer."

☐ a. Most people thought we were going to fail.

☐ b. Most people thought we were not religious.

☐ c. Many people prayed for us.

_____ Number of correct answers

Record your personal assessment of your work on the Critical Thinking Chart on page 150.

Critical Thinking

Follow the directions provided for questions 1, 3, and 4. Put an X in the box next to the correct answer for the other questions.

1. For each statement below, write O if it expresses an opinion or write F if it expresses a fact.

_____ a. A father of three children should not have risked his life climbing a mountain.

_____ b. Mount Everest is the tallest mountain on Earth.

_____ c. Many people would like to know whether Mallory and Irvine made it to the top of Mount Everest.

2. From the information in paragraph 8, you can predict that people will

☐ a. continue to search for Mallory's camera.

☐ b. soon forget about Mallory and Irvine.

☐ c. decide that finding the camera is not important, now that Mallory's body has been found.

3. Choose from the letters below to correctly complete the following statement. Write the letters on the lines.

In the article, _____ and _____ are alike.

   a. the reason Edmund Hillary and Tenzing Norgay climbed Mount Everest

   b. the reason George Mallory and Andrew Irvine climbed Mount Everest

   c. the reason Eric Simonson climbed Mount Everest

4. Read paragraph 16. Then choose from the letters below to correctly complete the following statement. Write the letters on the lines.

According to paragraph 16, _____ because _____.

   a. Mallory fell nearly a thousand feet

   b. searchers decided that Mallory had been climbing at night

   c. Mallory's sunglasses were in his pocket

5. What did you have to do to answer question 4?

☐ a. find a comparison (how things are the same)

☐ b. find a description (how something looks)

☐ c. find a cause (why something happened)

_____ Number of correct answers

Record your personal assessment of your work on the Critical Thinking Chart on page 150.

Personal Response

What would you have done next if you had been the one to find George Mallory's body on Mount Everest?

_____

_____

_____

_____

Self-Assessment

While reading the article, I found it easiest to _____

_____

_____

_____

Did Anastasia Survive?

It was a brutal and bloody scene. The guards told the family to go to the cellar. There Yakov Yurovsky, the head guard, ordered them to line up in two rows along a wall. The family members did as they were told. The mother and her son sat in front. The father and daughters stood behind. None of them had any idea what was about to happen. Yurovsky called in 11 guards armed with guns. Only then did the family realize they were about to be killed.

The Romanov family gathered for this photo shortly before the Russian Revolution in 1917. Maria stands next to her mother, Empress Alexandra. In the front row are Olga, Czar Nicholas II, Anastasia, Grand Duke Alexei, and Tatiana.

2   The guards opened fire. Some members of the family fell with the first volley. But others proved harder to kill. Bullets bounced off several of the children's bodies. These bullets ricocheted wildly around the small room. Again and again the guards fired their guns. Still, the bullets seemed to have no effect. (The reason was discovered later. Hundreds of family jewels had been sewed into the children's belts and underwear.) Frustrated, the guards moved in with rifle butts and bayonets to finish the job.

3   These gruesome events took place on July 17, 1918. They occurred in a small mining town in a remote part of Russia. The victims were the Romanovs. They were not just an ordinary family. They were the royal family of Russia. The father was czar, or emperor, of the whole country. His name was Nicholas II. On the day of the murders, Nicholas was with his wife, son, and four daughters. Their personal doctor and three servants were also with them.

4   The killings came after the family had been held prisoner for many days. Their captors were communists. These communists had overthrown Czar Nicholas II and taken charge of the country. At first they weren't sure what to do with the royal family. For 78 days they held them captive. Only then did they decide to kill them. The reason? Troops faithful to Nicholas were in the area. The communists feared the troops might try to rescue him.

5   After killing Nicholas and his family, the communists hurried to get rid of the bodies. They didn't want anyone to find them, ever. So first they burned them. Next they poured acid on them. Then they threw the bodies down a flooded mine shaft.

6   Somehow, though, the secret got out. People in the region heard stories of the murders. Frightened, Yurovsky sent men to recover the bodies. He told them to bury the bodies somewhere else.

7   For a long time the whereabouts of the Romanovs' bodies remained a mystery. Some people questioned whether the whole family really had been killed. Perhaps, they thought, one or two children had survived. The communists freely admitted they had killed Nicholas. But they were ashamed

to admit they had shot the rest of the family. So rumors swirled. Some Russians clung to the hope that one or two of the young Romanovs had lived.

8 After a while imposters started showing up. Each claimed to be a son or daughter of Nicholas II. Most of these people were exposed as phonies. But one young woman was not so easy to dismiss. Known as Anna Anderson, she seemed to be the real thing.

9 Anderson said that she was Anastasia, the czar's youngest daughter. Her tale went like this: She had not been killed that awful night in the cellar. Instead, she had fainted when the bullets started to fly. A friendly soldier rescued her. Together they fled to Germany. There the soldier left her. Miserable and alone, she tried to drown herself in 1920. She was saved when someone dragged her out of the river.

10 At that point no one knew who she was. She carried no purse, no papers. She would not tell anyone her name. Police put her in a hospital for the mentally ill. There, a worker saw an old photo of the Grand Duchess Anastasia. The worker compared the photo with the suicidal young patient called Anna Anderson. The two looked a lot alike. Was Anna Anderson in fact Anastasia?

11 For months, Anderson refused to answer that question. Then in 1921 she broke her silence. "I am the Grand Duchess Anastasia," she declared. Her claim was made stronger when she gave details that no one but a Romanov would know. For instance, she knew about a secret meeting that Nicholas had held with a German leader. Also, many agreed that her handwriting matched that of Anastasia. So did her mouth, her ears, her eyes. Everything about her seemed to confirm that she was Nicholas's youngest daughter. Later, friends of the royal family went to see her. They came away convinced that Anna Anderson was indeed Anastasia. For the rest of her life, Anderson stuck to her story. She died in 1984, still insisting she was Anastasia.

12 Meanwhile, in 1979 the bones of the dead Romanovs were found. A Russian writer named Geli Ryabov learned where they were buried. Ryabov did not dare tell anyone, though. The communists were still in power. Ryabov did not want to anger them by reminding the world of their hideous deeds.

13 So Ryabov dug up the bones secretly, at night. "It was just mind-boggling," he later said. "It was hard to believe, these black and green bones with signs of the burns from acid. One of the skulls had a bullet hole it."

14 By 1988 the old communists were out of power. Finally Ryabov came forward with the bones. Scientists performed tests to find out whose bones they were. The tests proved the bones belonged to the Romanovs.

15 Did that mean Anna Anderson had been a fake? Not necessarily. Two sets of Romanov bones were missing. There was no trace of Nicholas's son Alexei. There was no sign of Anastasia's bones, either. Some people took this as further proof that the two children had escaped. It made them more certain than ever that Anna Anderson had been telling the truth.

16 At last, in 1994 that part of the mystery was solved. A new test was done on the remains of Anna Anderson. The results were clear.

17 Anna Anderson's genes did not match those of the royal family. She was not Anastasia. After all those years, Anderson turned out to be as phony as the rest.

If you have been timed while reading this article, enter your reading time below. Then turn to the Words-per-Minute Table on page 147 and look up your reading speed (words per minute). Enter your reading speed on the graph on page 148.

Reading Time: Lesson 15

——— : ———

Minutes   Seconds

A Finding the Main Idea

One statement below expresses the main idea of the article. One statement is too general, or too broad. The other statement explains only part of the article; it is too narrow. Label the statements using the following key:

M—Main Idea   B—Too Broad   N—Too Narrow

_____ 1. For years, secrecy and mystery have surrounded the violent deaths of the Romanov family in Russia and have led to claims by imposters.

_____ 2. Often, when a group takes over a country by force, innocent people are killed.

_____ 3. Anna Anderson's mouth, ears, and eyes resembled those of Anastasia, the daughter of the czar, and her handwriting matched Anastasia's too.

_____ Score 15 points for a correct M answer.

_____ Score 5 points for each correct B or N answer.

_____ **Total Score:** Finding the Main Idea

B Recalling Facts

How well do you remember the facts in the article? Put an X in the box next to the answer that correctly completes each statement about the article.

1. The execution of the Romanovs took place
   ☐ a. in a remote part of Russia.
   ☐ b. in Poland.
   ☐ c. on a secluded farm in France.

2. It was difficult to kill the children because
   ☐ a. their parents stood in front of them.
   ☐ b. they were so cute.
   ☐ c. bullets ricocheted off the jewels sewn into their clothes.

3. Anna said that she had escaped death by
   ☐ a. fighting back.
   ☐ b. fainting and seeming to be dead.
   ☐ c. hiding in another room.

4. Police, who didn't know who Anna was,
   ☐ a. put her in jail.
   ☐ b. let her go free again.
   ☐ c. put her in a hospital for the mentally ill.

5. Anna could not have been a Romanov because
   ☐ a. her genes did not match those of the Romanovs.
   ☐ b. she did not remember important facts.
   ☐ c. she did not look like the Romanovs.

Score 5 points for each correct answer.

_____ **Total Score:** Recalling Facts

C | Making Inferences

When you combine your own experience and information from a text to draw a conclusion that is not directly stated in that text, you are making an inference. Below are five statements that may or may not be inferences based on information in the article. Label the statements using the following key:

C—Correct Inference   F—Faulty Inference

_____ 1. The Romanov parents thought that their children had a better chance to escape than they had.

_____ 2. The communists killed the entire family so they could brag about it to their allies.

_____ 3. The hospital worker who first said that Anna looked like Anastasia was part of the hoax.

_____ 4. It is possible to discover whether one person is related to another by comparing their genes.

_____ 5. The only reason that Anna Anderson pretended to be Anastasia was so that she could become rich.

Score 5 points for each correct answer.

_____ **Total Score:** Making Inferences

D | Using Words Precisely

Each numbered sentence below contains an underlined word or phrase from the article. Following the sentence are three definitions. One definition is closest to the meaning of the underlined word. One definition is opposite or nearly opposite. Label those two definitions using the following key; do not label the remaining definition.

C—Closest   O—Opposite or Nearly Opposite

1. These bullets ricocheted wildly around the small room.

_____ a. exploded

_____ b. bounced back and forth

_____ c. traveled in a straight line

2. For 78 days they held them captive.

_____ a. prisoner

_____ b. without talking

_____ c. free

3. After a while imposters started showing up.

_____ a. correctly identified people

_____ b. fakes

_____ c. relatives

4. The worker compared the photo with the suicidal young patient called Anna Anderson.

_____ a. thin

_____ b. eager to live life fully

_____ c. ready to end her own life

5. "It was just <u>mind-boggling</u>," he later said.

_____ a. astounding

_____ b. routine; dull

_____ c. sparkling

_____ Score 3 points for each correct C answer.

_____ Score 2 points for each correct O answer.

_____ **Total Score:** Using Words Precisely

Enter the four total scores in the spaces below, and add them together to find your Reading Comprehension Score. Then record your score on the graph on page 149.

Score	Question Type	Lesson 15
_____	Finding the Main Idea	
_____	Recalling Facts	
_____	Making Inferences	
_____	Using Words Precisely	
_____	**Reading Comprehension Score**	

Author's Approach

Put an X in the box next to the correct answer.

1. What do the authors mean by the statement "Frustrated, the guards moved in with rifle butts and bayonets to finish the job"?

☐ a. The frustrated guards were forced to move into the place where weapons were stored in order to finish the killings.

☐ b. The fact that the family could not be killed with rifle butts or bayonets frustrated the guards.

☐ c. The frustrated guards killed the remaining survivors using rifle butts and bayonets.

2. Choose the statement below that is the weakest argument for believing that Anna Anderson was Anastasia.

☐ a. Anna Anderson knew details that no one but a Romanov could know.

☐ b. Anna Anderson's genes did not match those of the royal family.

☐ c. Anna Anderson looked quite a bit like Anastasia.

3. The authors probably wrote this article to

☐ a. prove that people can no longer pretend to be someone else, now that genetic testing is available.

☐ b. persuade readers to hate communism.

☐ c. inform the reader about a famous historical mystery.

_____ Number of correct answers

Record your personal assessment of your work on the Critical Thinking Chart on page 150.

Summarizing and Paraphrasing

Follow the directions provided for questions 1 and 2. Put an X in the box next to the correct answer for question 3.

1. Look for the important ideas and events in paragraphs 5 and 6. Summarize those paragraphs in one or two sentences.

_____

_____

_____

2. Complete the following one-sentence summary of the article using the lettered phrases from the phrase bank below. Write the letters on the lines.

> **Phrase Bank**
> a. facts about Anna Anderson and a discussion about the mystery of where Anastasia and Alexei are buried
> b. the execution of the Romanov family
> c. why some people thought that Anna Anderson was Anastasia

The article "Did Anastasia Survive?" begins with _____,

goes on to explain _____, and ends with _____.

3. Read the statement from the article below. Then read the paraphrase of that statement. Choose the reason that best tells why the paraphrase does not say the same thing as the statement.

Statement: The worker compared the photo with the suicidal young patient called Anna Anderson.

Paraphrase: The worker showed the photo to a young patient who had tried to commit suicide.

☐ a. Paraphrase says too much.

☐ b. Paraphrase doesn't say enough.

☐ c. Paraphrase doesn't agree with the statement.

> _____ Number of correct answers
>
> Record your personal assessment of your work on the Critical Thinking Chart on page 150.

Critical Thinking

Follow the directions provided for questions 1, 2, and 3. Put an X in the box next to the correct answer for question 4.

1. For each statement below, write O if it expresses an opinion or write F if it expresses a fact.

_____ a. Anna Anderson convinced many people that she was Anastasia.

_____ b. People who don't accept that Anastasia is dead are just being stubborn.

_____ c. Killing the entire Romanov family was a cruel and cowardly act.

2. Using what you know about Anastasia and what is told about Anna Anderson in the article, name three ways Anna Anderson was similar to Anastasia and three ways she was different. Cite the paragraph number(s) where you found details in the article to support your conclusions.

Similarities

_____

_____

_____

Differences

_____

_____

_____

3. Reread paragraph 2. Then choose from the letters below to correctly complete the following statement. Write the letters on the lines.

According to paragraph 2, _____ because _____.

a. bullets seemed to have no effect on some of the Romanov children

b. some family members died after the first round of bullets

c. jewels had been sewed into their clothes

4. What did you have to do to answer question 2?

☐ a. find an opinion (what someone thinks about something)

☐ b. find a description (how something looks)

☐ c. find a contrast (how things are different)

_____ Number of correct answers

Record your personal assessment of your work on the Critical Thinking Chart on page 150.

Personal Response

Why do you think Anna Anderson said that she was Anastasia?

_____

_____

_____

Self-Assessment

Which concepts or ideas from the article were difficult to understand?

_____

_____

Which were easy?

_____

_____

Compare and Contrast

Think about the articles you have read in Unit Three. Pick three articles that tell about a tragic ending. Write the titles of the articles in the first column of the chart below. Use information you learned from the articles to fill in the empy boxes in the chart.

Title	Who suffered a tragedy in this story?	What happened to the victim of the tragedy?	Why do people still talk about this tragedy?

The article that I think was saddest was _____. I chose this article because _____

_____

_____

Words-per-Minute Table

Unit Three

Directions: If you were timed while reading an article, refer to the Reading Time you recorded in the box at the end of the article. Use this words-per-minute table to determine your reading speed for that article. Then plot your reading speed on the graph on page 148.

Lesson No. of Words	11 1,090	12 1,149	13 1,057	14 1,190	15 1,037	
1:30	727	766	705	793	691	**90**
1:40	654	689	634	714	622	**100**
1:50	595	627	577	649	566	**110**
2:00	545	575	529	595	519	**120**
2:10	503	530	488	549	479	**130**
2:20	467	492	453	510	444	**140**
2:30	436	460	423	476	415	**150**
2:40	409	431	396	446	389	**160**
2:50	385	406	373	420	366	**170**
3:00	363	383	352	397	346	**180**
3:10	344	363	334	376	327	**190**
3:20	327	345	317	357	311	**200**
3:30	311	328	302	340	296	**210**
3:40	297	313	288	325	283	**220**
3:50	284	300	276	310	271	**230**
4:00	273	287	264	298	259	**240**
4:10	262	276	254	286	249	**250**
4:20	252	265	244	275	239	**260**
4:30	242	255	235	264	230	**270**
4:40	234	246	227	255	222	**280**
4:50	226	238	219	246	215	**290**
5:00	218	230	211	238	207	**300**
5:10	211	222	205	230	201	**310**
5:20	204	215	198	223	194	**320**
5:30	198	209	192	793	189	**330**
5:40	192	203	187	210	183	**340**
5:50	187	197	181	204	178	**350**
6:00	182	192	176	198	173	**360**
6:10	177	186	171	193	168	**370**
6:20	172	181	167	714	164	**380**
6:30	168	177	163	183	160	**390**
6:40	164	172	159	179	156	**400**
6:50	160	168	155	174	152	**410**
7:00	156	164	151	170	148	**420**
7:10	152	160	147	166	145	**430**
7:20	149	157	144	162	141	**440**
7:30	145	153	141	159	138	**450**
7:40	142	150	138	155	135	**460**
7:50	139	147	135	152	132	**470**
8:00	136	144	132	149	130	**480**

Minutes and Seconds

Seconds

Plotting Your Progress: Reading Speed

Unit Three

Directions: If you were timed while reading an article, write your words-per-minute rate for that article in the box under the number of the lesson. Then plot your reading speed on the graph by putting a small X on the line directly above the number of the lesson, across from the number of words per minute you read. As you mark your speed for each lesson, graph your progress by drawing a line to connect the X's.

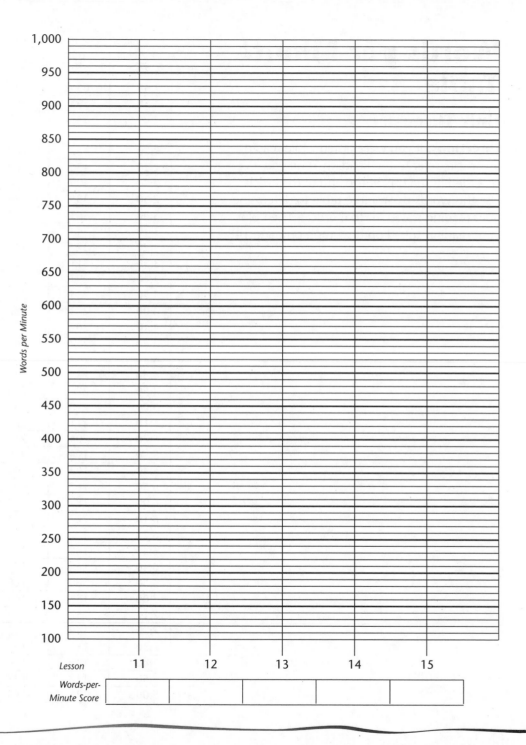

Words per Minute

Lesson: 11 12 13 14 15

Words-per-Minute Score

Plotting Your Progress: Reading Comprehension

Unit Three

Directions: Write your Reading Comprehension score for each lesson in the box under the number of the lesson. Then plot your score on the graph by putting a small X on the line directly above the number of the lesson and across from the score you earned. As you mark your score for each lesson, graph your progress by drawing a line to connect the X's.

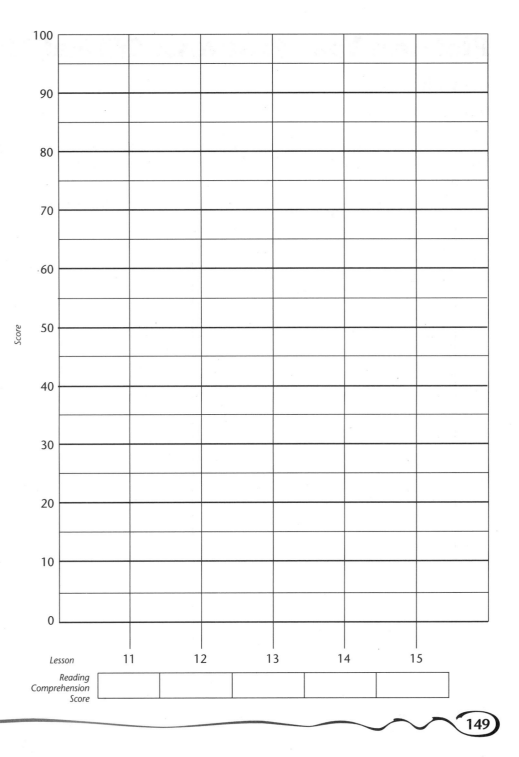

Plotting Your Progress: Critical Thinking

Unit Three

Directions: Work with your teacher to evaluate your responses to the Critical Thinking questions for each lesson. Then fill in the appropriate spaces in the chart below. For each lesson and each type of Critical Thinking question, do the following: Mark a minus sign (–) in the box to indicate areas in which you feel you could improve. Mark a plus sign (+) to indicate areas in which you feel you did well. Mark a minus-slash-plus sign (–/+) to indicate areas in which you had mixed success. Then write any comments you have about your performance, including ideas for improvement.

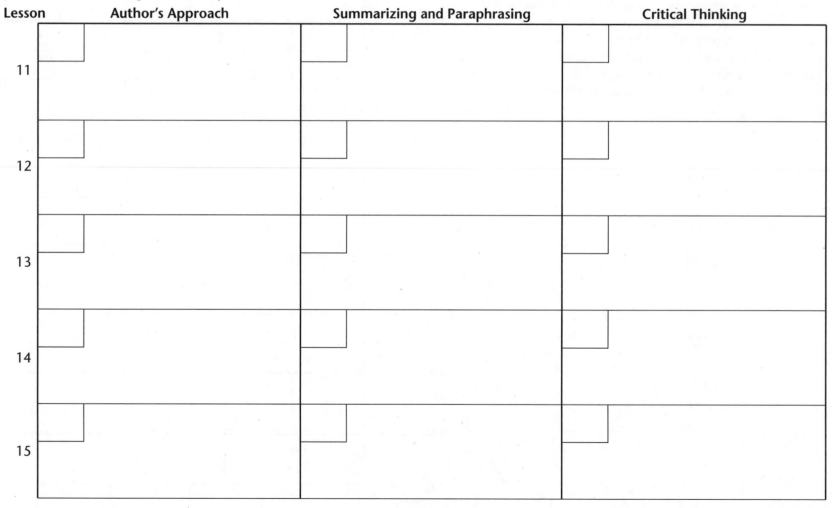

Lesson	Author's Approach	Summarizing and Paraphrasing	Critical Thinking
11			
12			
13			
14			
15			

Photo Credits